A Sage's Fruit

Essays of Baal HaSulam

Laitman
Kabbalah
Publishers

Yehuda Leib HaLevi Ashlag

A Sage's Fruit: essays of Baal HaSulam
Copyright © 2015 by Michael Laitman

All rights reserved
Published by Laitman Kabbalah Publishers
www.kabbalah.info   info@kabbalah.info
1057 Steeles Avenue West, Suite 532, Toronto, ON,
M2R 3X1, Canada
2009 85th Street #51, Brooklyn, New York, 11214, USA

Printed in Canada

ISBN: 978-1-77228-007-4

Library of Congress Control Number: 2015944046

Translation: Chaim Ratz
Editor: Mary Pennock
Proofreading: Noga Burnot, Mary Miesem
Layout: Chaim Ratz
Cover: Inna Smirnova
Executive Editor: Chaim Ratz
Printing and Post Production: Uri Laitman

FIRST EDITION: OCTOBER 2015
First printing

Table of Contents

To the Reader..5

Introduction...7

The Freedom...15

One Commandment. 49

Body and Soul..57

Peace in the World...65

The Love of God and the Love of Man...............................87

One Mitzva (Commandment). 91

Exile and Redemption. 101

Thou Hast Hemmed Me in Behind and Before. 107

Remembering..119

The Meaning of the Chaf in Anochi..................................135

The Wisdom of Israel Compared to External Wisdoms. 143

Four Worlds. 149

The Teaching of the Kabbalah and Its Essence....................155

The Wisdom of Kabbalah and Philosophy. 183

The Quality of the Wisdom of the Hidden in General........197

The Meaning of Conception and Birth. 209

From My Flesh I Shall See God..229

Inheritance of the Land...241

600,000 Souls. 245

Not the Time for the Livestock to Be Gathered...................251

Concealment and Disclosure of the Face
of the Creator (A). 257

Concealment and Disclosure of the Face
of the Creator (B)... 261

Further Reading.. 265

Further Reading.. 265

Contact Information 272

To the Reader

Rav Yehuda Ashlag, known as Baal HaSulam (Owner of the Ladder) for his *Sulam* (Ladder) commentary on *The Book of Zohar*, has written numerous essays, treatises, and other compositions. The essays in this book are some of the most notable and oft-studied among them.

For over sixty years, these texts have been sealed and concealed. Some of them have been affected by time; in some, the text has become indiscernible and the letters barely readable; in some, the text has been torn and some was lost.

Despite the great labor, mistakes are not unlikely. Ellipses are also quite common, either because the original text is incomplete, or because it cannot be read with certainty. All the writings in this book, save for the introductions, were written by Baal HaSulam and are published for the first time in English.

The Editor

Introduction

Introduction by the author's son

Sunday, *Kislev* 1, *TASHMA*, November 25, 1984.
"And behold a ladder set up on the earth, and the top of it
reached to heaven."

Let the friends rejoice and the complete be merry. Beloved friends will exult when they see delightful things, words that my father and teacher, of blessed memory, wrote.

And here I come to praise my father and teacher, whose holy words shine in our generation, the generation of darkness and concealment. And concerning the concealment and revelation, I heard from him, the holy one, on the eve of *Sukkot*, 1942, in Jerusalem, when he entered the *Sukkah* to see if it was properly built.

He said that there are two discernments in a *Sukkah*: 1) **Cloud**, 2) **Waste of barn and winery**. And he explained:

1. Cloud is concealment, like a cloud hiding the sun. If one can prevail over the cloud, he is rewarded with **a cloud of honor**, which is **an awakening from Above**.

This is considered MAN *de Ima*, applied during the 6,000 years, which is considered *Sod* (secret), when one has not yet achieved the nature called *Peshat* (literal). The discernment of cloud of honor arrives by an **awakening from Above**. This is considered **the seventh millennium, with respect to the 6,000**

7

years, which is when one has been personally rewarded, as it is known that general and particular are always the same. But this is called "MAN *de Ima*, clouds of honor."

2. Waste of barn and winery is considered MAN *de Malchut*, **sweetened precisely by faith**, called "**an awakening from below.**" This is so when a person is himself naturally capable. This is called MAN *de Nukva*, and it is considered "**the seventh millennium**," called "and one ruined" (as our sages said, "the world exists for 6,000 years, and one ruined"), since she has nothing of her own, which is *Malchut*.

Thus, there is a discernment of the **seventh millennium**, which is the **one ruined**, and there is a discernment of barn and winery, which is **nature**, meaning by oneself. And precisely if one is capable of receiving the abundance, he receives it.

But one can obtain the clouds of honor, which is the awakening from Above, **Above nature**, even if one is not fit. This is because the abundance comes from the Upper One, as in, "I am the Lord, that dwelleth with them in the midst of their uncleannesses."

And if one corrects the discernment of waste of barn and winery, the discernment of *Malchut*, MAN *de Nukva*, considered the **seventh millennium**, one is rewarded with the **tenth millennium**, considered GAR. Such a soul comes down to the world **once every ten generations**. Thus far the content of his holy words.

From these holy words we can understand the greatness of the soul of my father and teacher, and his degree while saying them. He had told me several times that he had never said words of Torah without first attaining the words of Torah from inside the degree.

But to somewhat understand his words, we should explain that there is the issue of the association of *Midat ha Rachamim* with *Din* (association of the quality of mercy with judgment), called *MAN de Ima*. This is considered *Bina*, which are vessels of bestowal, meaning a correction of association with *Midat ha Rachamim* took place, so the lower ones can achieve a complete measure, as presented in the "Preface to the Wisdom of Kabbalah" (Item 58). If man had been made of *Malchut* alone, called *Midat ha Din*, he would not be able to correct his actions whatsoever, since he would have no sparks of bestowal and he would be as the beasts, which have nothing in the form of bestowal.

For this reason, He preceded *Midat ha Rachamim*, which is *Bina*, to *Midat ha Din*, which is *Malchut*. Thus, it became possible for man's *Guf* (body), which emerged from *Behina Dalet*, to be included with the quality of bestowal, too.

And through the association of *Midat ha Rachamim* with *Din*, *Tzimtzum Bet* (second restriction) occurred, where only six *Sefirot*—called **6,000 years**—could shine. But *Tzimtzum Bet* will be cancelled in the **seventh millennium** and all ten *Sefirot* will shine in the degree once more. This is called "**the tenth millennium**," since all ten *Sefirot* shine in it, meaning the first three, as well.

However, in the **6,000 years**, called *VAK*, the degrees were divided, meaning only six *Sefirot*—called *HBD HGT de* (of) *Kelim* (vessels)—could shine, and in them only *HGT NHY* of Lights. This shone in the world of *Nekudim* during the *Katnut*. Subsequently, when *Gadlut* shone and *Tzimtzum Bet* was cancelled, they did not have the strength to receive the Lights in order to bestow, and they broke, since they were in order to receive.

The Ari wrote in *The Tree of Life, Shaar HaNekudim*, that the reason for the breaking was that there were great Lights and small *Kelim* that could not tolerate the Light. And Baal HaSulam interprets in *Talmud Eser Sefirot*, Part 7: Since the Light was so great that they could not receive it in order to bestow, and hence broke.

For this reason, the Ari says that **Kelim de Panim** and **Kelim de Achoraim** broke together and mingled with each other. From among the *Kelim* that broke, some *Kelim* can be sorted, and those are sorted and corrected through the world of *Atzilut*.

He also says that what is sorted is only *Kelim de* **Panim**, from which the *Katnut de Atzilut* emerged. The *Gadlut de Atzilut* sort only the *Kelim de Panim* that were incorporated in *Kelim de Achoraim*, but *Malchut* herself was concealed in *RADLA*.

He explained there that **Kelim de Panim** are vessels of bestowal, and only *Ohr Hassadim* can shine in these *Kelim*. It is called *Katnut*, since *HBD HGT de Kelim* shine in the degree, as well as *HGT NHY* of Lights, lacking *NHY de Kelim* and *GAR* of Lights.

Kelim de Achoraim are called "vessels of **reception**" because they need *Ohr Hochma*, called "Lights of GAR," which are Lights of *Gadlut*.

The Ari said that these *Kelim* will not be sorted during the 6,000 years. This is the meaning of the *Malchut* that was concealed in *RADLA*.

In "Inner Reflection," he asks, "If there are no vessels of **reception** there, how is there *Gadlut*," which is **Ohr Hochma** in *Atzilut*? He replies that *Gadlut de Atzilut* is really not from *Kelim de Achoraim*. Rather, *Gadlut de Atzilut* are vessels of bestowal with respect to the fact that they were **incorporated** with the *Kelim* of *Achoraim* when they broke and fell into *BYA*.

Hence, *Gadlut de* **Neshama** is from the *Kelim de Panim* that were integrated with the *Kelim de Achoraim* that remained in **Beria**. And **Ohr Haya** shines in **Atzilut** by sorting the *Kelim de Panim* that were included in *Yetzira*. And when the *Kelim* that were included in *Assiya* are sorted, **Mochin de Yechida** flows into the world of *Atzilut*.

However, **the seventh millennium is called "one ruined,"** meaning that *Tzimtzum Bet* is cancelled and all ten *Sefirot*

will shine. But **the seventh millennium, with respect to the 6,000 years,** is not called "one ruined," since *Tzimtzum Bet* is not cancelled but remains, and *Gadlut de Atzilut* is only through the rising of the vessels of reception to the place of *Atzilut*.

It turns out that *BYA*, in their place outside, due to *Tzimtzum Bet*, are still restricted, and the ten *Sefirot* shine only in the place of *Kelim de Panim*, called "the place of *Atzilut*."

According to the above, we can interpret that **the seventh millennium is the GAR that shines in the 6,000 years.** This is his intention in saying that there is a seventh millennium with respect to the 6,000 years, etc., and it is called **MAN de Ima**, meaning *Kelim de Panim*, which are vessels of **bestowal** that extend GAR in order to complete the ten *Sefirot*. This is called "raised *AHP*."

And we can interpret *Ima* being considered awakening from Above by the words of the Ari in *Mavo She'arim* (Gate 2, Part 3, Chapter 9): In the first time, the *Mayin Nukvin* rose not through ZON in *AVI*, etc.

And Baal HaSulam interprets that since *AHP de AVI* are placed in GE *de ZON*, when the Upper One elevates its *AHP*, GE *de ZON* rise, as well.

This is called "an awakening from Above," done by the Upper One, but ZON cannot rise by themselves.

And when the lower one rises to the Upper One, it receives bestowal there, which is considered Upper One, being the association of *Midat ha Rachamim* with *Din*. This is so because *Malchut, Midat ha Din,* was intergraded with *Bina, Midat ha Rachamim,* which is vessels of bestowal—the quality of the Creator, who is entirely to bestow.

It therefore follows that receiving the vessels of bestowal is through the Upper One. And this is called "**an awakening from Above,**" meaning that the **Upper One raises the lower one to** receive **Kelim de Bina**, which is vessels of bestowal, called *Midat ha Rachamim.*

Then, in the second time, after he already has vessels of bestowal, he **rises by himself** to receive vessels of reception, called **Midat ha Din**, and this is called **"an awakening from below."** Through it, he attains GAR, called **"the seventh millennium."**

But this is not really the seventh millennium, since *Malchut* was hidden in *RADLA*. Rather, it is the seventh millennium with respect to the **six thousand years**, which is still MAN *de Ima*, called **"Malchut sweetened in Bina."**

This is what is written in *The Zohar* (*Beresheet*, Part 2, p 152, Item 171): "Because of it, he said, 'See now that I am that I am, and there is no God besides me, from which to take advice,' for He has neither a second nor a partner," etc.

And Baal HaSulam interprets in *The Sulam* with these words: "At *Gmar Tikkun*, when the words 'become the chief corner-stone' are revealed, it will be said, 'See now that **I am that I am.**' *Malchut* is called '**I am**,' and since *Malchut* of *Tzimtzum Aleph* will receive the great *Zivug*, it will be revealed in the world that **I am** of the 6,000 years, which was associated with *Midat ha Rachamim*, and whose self was hidden, is **I**, meaning the I of *Tzimtzum Aleph*. This is the disclosure of *Malchut's* self, **and there is no God besides me, from which to take advice.**

"This is so because the I that is revealed in the 6,000 thousand years needed a second degree, meaning *Bina*, from which to receive counsel, meaning correction. But now I do not need advice from another because I provide for all my needs by myself, **or a partner**, for I am no longer associated with *Midat ha Rachamim*, since my *Din* is mitigated in the sweetness of perfection. **Or calculation**, meaning the *Masach* associated with *Midat ha Rachamim* of *Bina*, which is called 'calculation,' since *Heshbon* (calculation) comes from the word *Machshava* (thought/contemplation), which is the name of *Bina* that mitigates the *Masach* and says that now she no longer needs this calculation."

This is the difference between the **seventh millennium, with respect to the 6,000 years, and the 10th millennium.**

And what can we, who heed his teachings, reply after him, for we have been granted only a glimpse into his greatness. And how can we climb the mountain and touch his toes and even draw near his virtues? His innovations and his holy teachings shine today as in the day when they were first said.

This is the reason why I said that the day this book, the writings of my father and teacher, Baal HaSulam, has been revealed to the world is so great. May his holy words bring us close to walking in the ways of the work of God.

Baruch Shalom son of my father and teacher

Yehuda Leib HaLevi Ashlag of blessed memory

The Freedom

Freedom of Will / Pleasure and Pain / The Law of Causality / Four Factors / The Source, the First Matter / Cause and Effect that Stem from Itself / Internal Cause and Effect / Cause and Effect through Alien Things / Hereditary Possessions / Influence of the Environment / Habit Turns to Second Nature / External Factors / Free Choice / The Environment as a Factor / The Necessity to Choose a Good Environment / The Mind's Control over the Body / Freedom of the Individual / The General Shape of the Progenitor Is Never Lost / The Necessity of Preserving the Freedom of the Individual / The Will to Receive—Existence from Absence / Two Forces in the Will to Receive: Attracting Force and Rejecting Force / One Law for All the Worlds / Taking after the Collective / A Path of Torah and a Path of Pain / The Collective's Right to Expropriate the Freedom of the Individual / In Spiritual Life – the Law, "Take after the Individual" / Criticism Brings Success; Lack of Criticism Causes Decadence / Ancestral Heritage / Two Discernments: A) Potential, B) Actual / Two Creations: A) Man, B) A Living Soul /

"*Harut* (carved) on the stones"; do not pronounce it *Harut* (carved), but *Herut* (freedom), to show that they are liberated from the angel of death.

These words need to be clarified, because how is the matter of reception of the Torah related to one's liberation from death? Furthermore, once they have attained an eternal body that cannot die through the reception of the Torah, how did they lose it again? Can the eternal become absent?

Freedom of Will

To understand the sublime concept, "freedom from the angel of death," we must first understand the concept of freedom as it is normally understood by all of humanity.

It is a general view that freedom is deemed a natural law, which applies to all of life. Thus, we see that animals that fall into captivity die when we rob them of their freedom. This is a true testimony that Providence does not accept the enslavement of any creature. It is with good reason that humanity has been struggling for the past several hundred years to obtain a certain measure of freedom of the individual.

Yet, this concept, expressed in that word, "freedom," remains unclear, and if we delve into the meaning of that word, there will be almost nothing left. For before you seek the freedom of the individual, you must assume that any individual, in and of itself, has that quality called "freedom," meaning that one can act according to one's own free choice.

Pleasure and Pain

However, when we examine the acts of an individual, we shall find them compulsory. He is compelled to do them and has no freedom of choice. In a sense, he is like a stew cooking on a stove; it has no choice but to cook. And it must cook because Providence has harnessed life with two chains: **pleasure and pain**.

The living creatures have no freedom of choice—to choose pain or reject pleasure. And man's advantage over animals is that he can aim at a remote goal, meaning to agree to a certain amount of current pain, out of choice of future benefit or pleasure, to be attained after some time.

But in fact, there is no more than a seemingly commercial calculation here, where the future benefit or pleasure seems preferable and advantageous to the agony they are suffering from the pain they have agreed to assume presently. There is only a matter of deduction here—that they deduct the pain and suffering from the anticipated pleasure, and there remains some surplus.

Thus, only the pleasure is extended. And so it sometimes happens that we are tormented because we did not find the attained pleasure to be the surplus we had hoped for compared to the agony we suffered; hence, we are in deficit, just as merchants do.

And when all is said and done, there is no difference here between man and animal. And if that is the case, there is no free choice whatsoever, but a pulling force, drawing them toward any bypassing pleasure and rejecting them from painful circumstances. And Providence leads them to every place it chooses by means of these two forces without asking their opinion in the matter.

Moreover, even determining the type of pleasure and benefit is entirely out of one's own free choice, but follow the will of others, as they want, and not he. For example: I sit, I dress, I speak, and I eat. I do all these not because I want to sit that way, or talk that way, or dress that way, or eat that way, but because others want me to sit, dress, talk, and eat that way. It all follows the desire and fancy of society, not my own free will.

Furthermore, in most cases, I do all these against my will. For I would be a lot more comfortable behaving simply, without any burden. But I am enslaved in all my movements, chained with iron shackles to the fancies and manners of others, which make up the society.

So you tell me, where is my freedom of will? On the other hand, if we assume that the will has no freedom, then we are all like machines, operating and creating through external forces that force them to act this way. This means that we are all incarcerated in the prison of Providence, which, using these two chains, pleasure and pain, pushes and pulls us to its will, to where it sees fit.

It turns out that there is no such thing as selfishness in the world, since no one here is free or stands on his own two feet. I am not the owner of the act, and I am not the performer because I want to perform, but I am performed upon, in a compulsory manner, and without my awareness. Thus, reward and punishment become extinct.

And it is quite odd not only for the orthodox, who believe in His Providence and can rely on Him and trust that He aims only for the best in this conduct. It is even stranger for those who believe in nature, since according to the above, we are all incarcerated by the chains of blind nature, with no awareness or accountability. And we, the chosen species, with reason and knowledge, have become a toy in the hands of the blind nature, which leads us astray, and who knows where?

THE LAW OF CAUSALITY

It is worthwhile taking some time to grasp such an important thing, meaning how we exist in the world as beings with a "self," where each of us regards himself a unique entity, acting on its own, independent of external, alien, and unknown forces. And does this being—the self—appear to us?

It is true that there is a general connection among all the elements of reality before us, which abide by the law of causality, by way of cause and effect, moving forward. And as the whole, so is each item for itself, meaning that each and every creature in the world from the four types—still, vegetative, animate, and speaking—abides by the law of causality by way of cause and effect.

Moreover, each particular form of a particular behavior, which a creature follows while in this world, is pushed by ancient causes, compelling it to accept that change in that behavior and not another whatsoever. And this is apparent to all who examine the ways of nature from a pure scientific point of view and without a shred of bias. Indeed, we must analyze this matter to allow ourselves to examine it from all sides.

FOUR FACTORS

Bear in mind that every emergence occurring in the beings of the world must be perceived not as extending existence from absence, but as existence from existence, through an actual entity that has shed its previous form and has robed its current one.

Therefore, we must understand that in every emergence in the world there are four factors where from the four of them together arises that emergence. They are called by the names:

A. The source.

B. The unchanging conduct of cause and effect related to the source's own attribute.

C. Its internal conducts of cause and effect, which change by contact with alien forces.

D. The conducts of cause and effect of alien things, which affect it from the outside.

And I will clarify them one at a time:

First Reason: the Source, the First Matter

A) The "source" is the first matter, related to that being. For "there is nothing new under the sun," and anything that happens in our world is not existence from absence, but existence from existence. It is an entity that has stripped off its former shape and taken on another form, different from the first. And that entity, which shed its previous form, is defined as "the source." In it lies the potential destined to be revealed and determined at the end of the formation of that emergence. Therefore, it is clearly considered its primary cause.

Second Reason: Cause and Effect that Stem from Itself

B) This is a conduct of cause and effect, related to the source's own attribute, and which is unchanging. Take, for example, a stalk of wheat that has rotted in the ground and arrived at a state of sowing many stalks of wheat. Thus, that rotten state is deemed the "source," meaning that the essence of the wheat has stripped off its former shape, the shape of wheat, and has taken on a new discernment, that of rotten wheat, which is the seed, called "the source," which has no shape at all. Now, after rotting in the ground, it has become fit for robing another form, the form of many stalks of wheat, intended to emerge from that source, which is the seed.

It is known to all that this source is destined to become neither cereal nor oats, but only equalize with its former shape, which has left it, being the single stalk of wheat. And although it changes to a certain degree in quality and quantity, for in the former shape it was a single stalk, and now there are ten stalks, and in taste and appearance, too, the essence of the shape of the wheat remains unchanged.

Thus, there is a conduct of cause and effect here, ascribed to the source's own attribute, which never changes. Thus, cereal will never emerge from wheat, as we have said, and this is called "the second reason."

Third Reason: Internal Cause and Effect

C) This is the conduct of the internal cause and effect of the source, which change upon encountering the alien forces in its environment. Thus, we find that from one stalk of wheat, which rots in the ground, many stalks emerge, sometimes larger and better wheat than prior to sowing.

Therefore, there must be additional factors involved here, collaborating and connecting with the force concealed in the environment, meaning the "source." And because of that, the additions in quality and quantity that were absent in the previous form of wheat have now appeared. Those are the minerals and the materials in the ground, the rain and the sun. All these operate on it by administering from their forces and joining the force within the source itself. And through the conduct of cause and effect, they have produced the multiplicity in quantity and quality in that emergence.

We must understand that this third factor joins with the internality of the source, since the force hidden in the source controls them. In the end, all these changes belong to the wheat and to no other plant. Hence, we define them as internal factors. However, they differ from the second factor, which is utterly unchanging, whereas the third factor changes in both quality and quantity.

Fourth Reason: Cause and Effect through Alien Things

This is a conduct of cause and effect of alien things that act upon it from the outside. In other words, they have no direct relation to the wheat, like minerals, rain, or sun, but are alien to it, such as nearby things or external events, such as hail, wind, etc.

And you find that four factors combine to the wheat throughout its growth. Each particular state that the wheat is subject to during that time becomes conditioned on the four of them, and the quality and quantity of each state is determined by them. And as we have portrayed in the wheat, so is the rule in every emergence in the world, even in thoughts and ideas.

If, for example, we picture to ourselves some conceptual state in a certain individual, such as a state of a person being religious or non religious, or an extreme orthodox or not so extreme, or midway, we will understand that that state is determined in that person by the above four factors.

Hereditary Possessions

The cause of the first reason is the source, which is its first substance. Man is created existence-from-existence, meaning from the minds of its progenitors. Thus, to a certain extent, it is like copying from book to book. This means that almost all the matters that were accepted and attained in the fathers and forefathers are copied here, as well.

But the difference is that they are in an abstract form, much like the sowed wheat, which is not fit for sowing until it has rotted and shed its former shape. So is the case with the drop of semen from which man is born: there is nothing in it of its forefathers' shapes, only abstract force.

For the same ideas that were concepts in his forefathers have turned into mere tendencies in him, called "qualities" or "habits," without even knowing why one does what he does. Indeed, they are hidden forces he had inherited from his ancestors in a way that not only do the material possessions come to us through inheritance from our ancestors, but the spiritual possessions and all the concepts that our fathers engaged in also come to us by inheritance from generation to generation.

And from here surface the manifold tendencies that we find in people, such as a tendency to believe or to criticize, a tendency to settle for material life or desiring only spiritual perfection, despising a life without aspirations, stingy, yielding, insolent, or shy.

All these pictures that appear in people are not their own property, which they have acquired, but mere inheritance that had been given to them by their ancestors. It is known that there is a special place in the brain where these hereditaments reside.

It is called, "the elongated brain," and all those tendencies appear there.

But because the concepts of our ancestors, acquired through their experiences, have become mere tendencies in us, they are considered the same as the sowed wheat, which has taken off its former shape and remained bare, having only potential forces worthy of receiving new forms. In our matter, these tendencies will robe the forms of concepts, which is therefore considered "the source."

Know, that some of these tendencies come in a negative form, meaning the opposite of the ones that were in his ancestors. This is why they said, "All that is concealed in the father's heart emerges openly in the son."

The reason for it is that the source takes off its former shape in order to take on a new form. Hence, it is close to losing the shapes of the concepts of his ancestors, like the wheat that rots in the ground loses the shape that existed in the wheat. However, it still depends on the other three factors.

INFLUENCE OF THE ENVIRONMENT

The second reason is an unchanging, direct conduct of cause and effect, related to the source's own attribute. Meaning, as we have clarified with the wheat that rots in the ground, the environment in which the source rests, as we have explained above, affect the sowing by a long chain of cause and effect in a long and gradual process, state by state, until they ripen.

And the source retakes its former shape, the shape of wheat, but differing in quality and quantity. In their general aspect, they remain completely unchanged; hence, no cereal or oats will grow from it. But in their particular aspect, they change in quantity, as from one stalk emerge a dozen or two dozen stalks, and in quality, as they are better or worse than the former shape of the wheat.

It is the same here: man, as a "source," is placed in an environment, meaning in the society. And he is necessarily affected by it, as the wheat from its environment, for the source is but a raw form. Thus, through the constant contact with the environment and the society, he is gradually impressed by them through a chain of consecutive states, one by one, as cause and effect.

At that time, the tendencies included in his source are changed and take on the form of concepts. For example, if one inherits from his ancestors a tendency to stinginess, as he grows he builds for himself concepts and ideas that conclude decisively that it is good for a person to be stingy. Thus, although his father was generous, he can inherit from him the negative tendency—to be stingy, for the absence is just as much inheritance as the presence.

Or, if one inherits from one's ancestors a tendency to be open-minded, he builds for himself ideas, and draws from them conclusions that it is good for a person to be open-minded. But where does one find those sentences and reasons? One takes all that from his environment unknowingly, for they impart to him their views and likings in the form of gradual cause and effect.

Hence, man regards them as his own possession, which he acquired through his free thought. But here, too, as with the wheat, there is one unchanging part of the source, for in the end, the tendencies he had inherited remain as they were in his forefathers. And this is called "the second factor."

HABIT TURNS TO SECOND NATURE

The third reason is a conduct of direct cause and effect, which affect the source and change it. Because the inherited tendencies in man have become concepts, due to the environment, they operate in the same directions that these concepts define. For example, a man of frugal nature, in whom the tendency for stinginess has been turned into a concept, through the environment, perceives frugality through some reasonable definition.

Let us assume that with this conduct he protects himself from needing others. Thus, he has acquired a scale for frugality, and when that fear is absent, he can waive it. Thus, he has substantially changed for the better from the tendency he had inherited from his forefathers. And sometimes one manages to completely uproot a bad tendency. This is done by habit, which has the ability to become a second nature.

In that, the strength of man is greater than that of a plant. For wheat can change only in its private part, as we have said above, whereas man has the ability to change through the cause and effect of the environment, even in the general parts, that is, to completely invert a tendency and uproot it to its opposite.

EXTERNAL FACTORS

The fourth reason is a conduct of cause and effect that affects the source by things that are completely alien to it, and operates on it from the outside. This means that these things are not at all related to the source's growth conduct, to affect it directly, but rather operate indirectly. For example, monetary issues, burdens, or the winds, etc., have their own complete, slow, and gradual order of states by way of "cause and effect," and change man's concepts for better or for worse.

Thus, I have set up the four natural factors that each thought and idea that appears in us is but their fruits. And even if one were to sit and contemplate something all day long, he will not be able to add or to alter what those four factors give him. Any addition he can add is in the quantity: whether a great intellect or a small one. But in the quality, he cannot add one bit. This is because they are the ones that compellingly determine the nature and shape of the idea and the conclusion without asking our opinion. Thus, we are at the hands of these four factors, as clay in the hands of a potter.

Free Choice

However, when we examine these four factors, we find that although our strength is not enough to face the first factor, the "source," we still have the ability and the free choice to protect ourselves against the other three factors, by which the source changes in its individual parts, and sometimes in its general part, as well, through habit, which endows it with a second nature, as has been explained above.

The Environment as a Factor

This protection means that we can always supplement in the matter of choosing our environment, which is the friends, books, teachers, and so on. It is like a person who inherited a few stalks of wheat from his father. From this small amount he can grow dozens of stalks through his choice of the environment for his "source," which is fertile soil, with all the necessary minerals and raw materials that nourish the wheat abundantly.

There is also the matter of the work of improving the environmental conditions to fit the needs of the plant and the growth, for the wise will do well to choose the best conditions and will find blessing. And the fool will take from whatever comes before him, and will thus turn the sowing to a curse rather than to a blessing.

Thus, all its praise and spirit depends on the choice of the environment in which to sow the wheat. But once it has been sown in the selected location, the wheat's absolute shape is determined according to the measure that the environment is capable of providing.

So is the case with our topic, for it is true that the desire has no freedom. Rather, it is operated by the above four factors. And one is compelled to think and examine as they suggest, denied of any strength to criticize or change, as the wheat that has been sown in its environment.

However, there is freedom for the will to initially choose such an environment, such books, and such guides that impart to him good concepts. If one does not do that, but is willing to enter any environment that appears to him and read any book that falls into his hands, he is bound to fall into a bad environment or waste his time on worthless books, which are abundant and easier to come by. In consequence, he will be forced into foul concepts that make him sin and condemn. **He will certainly be punished, not because of his evil thoughts or deeds, in which he has no choice, but because he did not choose to be in a good environment, for in that there is definitely a choice.**

Therefore, he who strives continually to choose a better environment is worthy of praise and reward. But here, too, it is not because of his good thoughts and deeds, which come to him without his choice, but because of his effort to acquire a good environment that brings him these good thoughts and deeds. It is as Rabbi Yehoshua Ben Perachya said, "Make for yourself a Rav, and buy for yourself a friend."

THE NECESSITY TO CHOOSE A GOOD ENVIRONMENT

Now you can understand the words of Rabbi Yosi Ben Kisma (*Avot* 86), who replied to a person who offered him to live in his town, and he would give him thousands of gold coins for it: "Even if you give me all the gold and silver and jewels in the world, I will live only in a place of Torah." These words seem too sublime for our simple mind to grasp, for how could he relinquish thousands of gold coins for such a small thing as living in a place where there are no disciples of Torah, while he himself was a great sage who needed to learn from no one? Indeed, a mystery.

But as we have seen, it is a simple thing, and should be observed by each and every one of us. For although everyone has "his own source," the forces are revealed openly only through the environment one is in. This is similar to the wheat sown in the ground, whose forces become apparent only through its environment, which is the soil, the rain, and the light of the sun.

Thus, Rabbi Yosi Ben Kisma correctly assumed that if he were to leave the good environment he had chosen and fall into a harmful environment, in a city where there is no Torah, not only would his former concepts be compromised, but all the other forces hidden in his source, which he had not yet revealed in action, would remain concealed. This is because they would not be subject to the right environment that would be able to activate them.

And as we have clarified above, **only in the matter of the choice of environment is man's reign over himself measured, and for this he should receive either reward or punishment.** Therefore, one must not wonder at a sage such as Rabbi Yosi Ben Kisma for choosing the good and declining the bad, and for not being tempted by material and corporeal things, as he deduces there: "When one dies, one does not take with him silver, or gold, or jewels, but only Torah and good deeds."

And so our sages warned, "Make for yourself a Rav, and buy for yourself a friend." And there is also the choice of books, as we have mentioned, for only in that is one rebuked or praised—in his choice of environment. But once he has chosen the environment, he is at its hands as clay in the hands of the potter.

THE MIND'S CONTROL OVER THE BODY

Some external contemporary sages, after contemplating the above matter and seeing how man's mind is but a fruit that grows out of the events of life, as we explained above, concluded that the mind has no control whatsoever over the body, but only life's events, imprinted in the physical tendons of the brain, control and activate man. And a man's mind is like a mirror, reflecting the shapes before it. And although the mirror is the carrier of these shapes, it cannot activate or move the shapes reflected in it.

So is the mind. Although life's events, in all their discernments of cause and effect, are seen and recognized by the mind, the mind is nonetheless utterly incapable of controlling the body, to bring it into motion, meaning to bring it closer to the good or remove it from the bad. This is because the spiritual and the physical are completely remote from one another, and there is no intermediary tool between them to enable the spiritual mind to activate and operate the corporeal body, as has been discussed at length.

But where they are smart, they disrupt. Man's imagination uses the mind just as the microscope serves the eye: without the microscope, he would not see anything harmful, due to its smallness. But once he has seen the harmful being through the microscope, man distances himself from the noxious factor.

Thus, it is the microscope that brings man to distance himself from the harm, and not the sense, for the sense did not detect the noxious factor. And to that extent, the mind fully controls man's body, to avert it from bad and bring it near the good. Thus, in all the places where the attribute of the body fails to recognize the beneficial or the detrimental, it needs only the mind's wit.

Furthermore, since man knows his mind, which is a true conclusion from life's experiences, **he can therefore receive knowledge and understanding from a trusted person and take it as law, although his life's events have not yet revealed these concepts to him.** It is like a person who asks the advice of a doctor and obeys him even though he understands nothing with his own mind. Thus, one uses the mind of others no less than one uses one's own.

As we have clarified above, there are two ways for Providence to make sure certain that man achieves the good, final goal: the path of pain and the path of Torah.

All the clarity that we have mentioned there, in the path of the Torah stems from that. For these clear conceptions that were revealed and recognized after a long chain of events in the lives of the prophets and the men of God, man comes and fully utilizes them and benefits from them, as though these concepts were events of his own life. Thus, you see that one is exempted from all the ordeals one must experience before he can develop that clear mind by himself. Thus, one saves both time and pain.

It can be compared to a sick man who does not wish to obey the doctor's orders before he understands by himself how that advice would cure him, and therefore begins to study medicine. He could die of his illness before he learns medicine.

So is the path of pain vs. the path of Torah. One who does not believe the concepts that the Torah and prophecy advise him to accept without self-understanding, must come to these conceptions by himself by following the chain of cause and effect from life's events. These are experiences that greatly rush, and can develop the sense of recognition of evil in them, as we have seen, without one's choice, but because of one's efforts to acquire a good environment, which leads to these thoughts and actions.

FREEDOM OF THE INDIVIDUAL

Now we have come to a thorough and accurate understanding of the freedom of the individual. However, that relates only to the first factor, the "source," which is the first substance of every person, meaning all the characteristics we inherit from our forefathers and by which we differ from each other.

This is because even when thousands of people share the same environment in such a way that the other three factors affect all of them equally, you will still not find two people who share the same attribute. This is because each of them has his/

her own source. This is like the source of the wheat: although it changes a great deal by the three remaining factors, it still retains the preliminary shape of wheat and will never take on the form of another species.

THE GENERAL SHAPE OF THE PROGENITOR IS NEVER LOST

So it is that each "source" that had taken off the preliminary shape of the progenitor and had taken on a new shape as a result of the three factors that were added to it, and which change it significantly, the general shape of the progenitor still remains, and will never assume the shape of another person who resembles him, just as oat will never resemble wheat.

This is so because each and every source has, in itself, a long sequence of generations comprised of several hundred generations, and the source includes the conceptions of them all. However, they are not revealed in it in the same ways they appeared in the ancestors, that is, in the form of ideas, but only as abstract forms. Therefore, they exist in him in the form of abstract forces called "natural tendencies," without knowing their reason or why he does what he does. Thus, there can never be two people with the same attribute.

THE NECESSITY OF PRESERVING THE FREEDOM OF THE INDIVIDUAL

Know, that this is the one true possession of the individual that must not be harmed or altered. This is because the end of all these tendencies, which are included in the source, is to materialize and assume the form of concepts when that individual grows and obtains a mind of his own, as a result of the law of evolution, which controls that chain and prompts it ever forward, as explained in the article "The Peace." Also, we learn that each and every tendency is bound to turn into a sublime and immeasurably important concept.

Thus, anyone who eradicates a tendency from an individual and uproots it causes the loss of that sublime and wondrous concept from the world, intended to emerge at the end of the chain, for that tendency will never again emerge in any other body. Accordingly, we must understand that when a particular tendency takes the form of a concept, it can no longer be distinguished as good or bad. This is because such distinctions are recognized only when they are still tendencies or immature concepts, and in no way are any of them recognized when they assume the shape of true concepts. This will be fully explained in the following articles.

From the above we learn what a terrible wrong inflict those nations that force their reign on minorities, depriving them of freedom without allowing them to live their lives by the tendencies they have inherited from their ancestors. They are regarded as no less than murderers.

And even those who do not believe in religion or in purposeful guidance can understand the necessity to preserve the freedom of the individual by watching nature's systems. For we can see how all the nations that ever fell, throughout the generations, came to it only due to their oppression of minorities and individuals, which had therefore rebelled against them and ruined them. Hence, it is clear to all that peace cannot exist in the world if we do not take into consideration the freedom of the individual. Without it, peace will not be sustainable and ruin will prevail.

Thus, we have clearly defined the essence of the individual with utmost accuracy, after the deduction of all that he takes from the public. But now we face a question: "Where, in the end, is the individual himself?" All we have said thus far concerning the individual is perceived as only the property of the individual, inherited from his ancestors. But where is the individual himself, the heir and the carrier of that property, who demands that we guard his property?

From all that has been said thus far, we have yet to find the point of "self" in man, which stands before us as an independent unit. And why do I need the first factor, which is a long chain of thousands of people, one after the other, from generation to generation, with which we set the image of the individual as an heir? And why do I need the other three factors, which are the thousands of people, standing one besides the other in the same generation? In the end, each individual is but a public machine, forever ready to serve the public as it sees fit. Meaning, he has become subordinate to two types of public: From the perspective of the first factor, he has become subordinate to a large public from past generations, standing one after the other; and from the perspective of the three other factors, he has become subordinate to his contemporary public.

This is indeed a universal question. For this reason, many oppose the above natural method, although they truly acknowledge its validity. Instead, they choose metaphysical methods, or dualism, or transcendentalism, to depict for themselves some spiritual object and how it sits within the body, in man's soul. And it is that soul that learns and that operates the body, and it is man's essence, his "self."

And perhaps these interpretations could ease the mind, but the problem is that they have no scientific solution as to how a spiritual object can have any contact with physical atoms to bring them into any kind of motion. All their wisdom and delving did not help them find a bridge on which to cross that wide and deep crevice that spreads between the spiritual entity and the corporeal atom. Thus, science has gained nothing from all these metaphysical methods.

The Will to Receive—Existence from Absence

To move a step forward in a scientific manner here, all we need is the wisdom of Kabbalah. This is because all the teachings in the world are included in the wisdom of Kabbalah. Concerning spiritual lights and vessels (*Panim Masbirot*, *The Tree of Life*, Branch 1), we learn that the primary innovation, from the perspective of Creation, which He has created existence from absence, applies to one aspect only, defined as the "will to receive." All other matters in the whole of Creation are not innovations at all; they are not existence from absence, but existence from existence. This means that they extend directly from His essence, as the light extends from the sun. There, too, there is nothing new, since what is found in the core of the sun extends outwardly.

However, the will to receive is complete novelty. Meaning, prior to Creation such a thing did not exist in reality, since He has no aspect of desire to receive, as He precedes everything, so from whom would He receive?

For this reason, this will to receive, which He extracted as existence from absence, is complete novelty. But all the rest is not considered an innovation that could be called "Creation." Hence, all the vessels and the bodies, both from spiritual worlds and from physical worlds, are deemed spiritual or corporeal substance, whose nature is the will to receive.

Two Forces in the Will to Receive: Attracting Force and Rejecting Force

You need to determine further that we distinguish two forces in that force called the "will to receive": the attracting force and the rejecting force.

The reason is that each body, or vessel, defined by the will to receive is indeed limited, meaning the quality it will receive and the quantity it will receive. Therefore, all the quantity and quality that are outside its boundaries appear to be against its nature; hence, it rejects them. Thus, that "will to receive," although it is deemed an attracting force, is compelled to become a rejecting force, as well.

ONE LAW FOR ALL THE WORLDS

Although the wisdom of Kabbalah mentions nothing of our corporeal world, there is still only one law for all the worlds (as written in the article, "The Essence of the Wisdom of Kabbalah," section, "The Law of Root and Branch"). Thus, all the corporeal entities in our world, that is, everything within that space, be it still, vegetative, animate, a spiritual object or a corporeal object, if we want to distinguish the unique, self aspect of each of them, how they differentiate from one another, even in the smallest of particles, it amounts to no more than the above mentioned "desire to receive." This is its entire particular form, from the perspective of the generated Creation, limiting it in quantity and quality. As a result, there is an attracting force and the rejecting force in it.

Yet, anything other that exists in it besides these two forces is deemed the bounty from His essence. That bounty is equal for all creatures, and it presents no innovation, with respect to Creation, as it extends existence from existence.

Also, it cannot be ascribed to any particular unit, but only to things that are common to all parts of Creation, small or large. Each of them receives from that bounty according to its will to receive, and this limitation defines each individual and unit.

Thus, I have evidently—from a purely scientific perspective—proven the "self" (ego) of every individual in a scientific, completely criticism-proof method, even according to the system of the fanatic, automatic materialists. From now on, we have no need for those lame methods dipped in metaphysics.

And of course, it makes no difference whether this force, being the will to receive, is a result and a fruit of the material that had produced it through chemistry, or that the material is a result and a fruit of that force. This is because we know that the main thing is that only this force, imprinted in every being and atom of the "will to receive," within its boundaries, is the unit where it is separated and distinguished from its environment. And this holds true both for a single atom or for a group of atoms, called "a body."

All other discernments in which there is a surplus of that force are not related in any way to that particle or that group of particles, with respect to itself, but only with respect to the whole, which is the bounty extended to them from the Creator, which is common to all parts of Creation together, without distinction of specific created bodies.

Now we shall understand the matter of the freedom of the individual, according to the definition of the first factor, which we called the "source," where all previous generations, which are the ancestors of that individual, have imprinted their nature, as we explained above. And as has been clarified, the meaning of the word, "individual," is but the boundaries of the will to receive, imprinted in its group of molecules.

Thus you see that all the tendencies he has inherited from his ancestors are indeed no more than boundaries of his will to receive, either related to the attracting force in him, or to the rejecting force in him, which appear before us as tendencies for stinginess or generosity, a tendency to mingle or to stay secluded, and so on.

Because of that, they really are his self (ego), fighting for its existence. Thus, if we eradicate even a single tendency from that individual, we are considered to be cutting off an actual organ from his essence. And it is also considered a genuine loss for all

Creation, because there is no other like it, nor will there ever be like it in the whole world.

After we have thoroughly clarified the just right of the individual according to the natural laws, let us turn and see just how practical it is, without compromising the theory of ethics and statesmanship. And most important: how this right is applied by our holy Torah.

TAKING AFTER THE COLLECTIVE

Our scriptures say: "Take after the collective." That means that wherever there is a dispute between the collective and the individual, we are obliged to rule according to the will of the collective. Thus, you see that the collective has a right to expropriate the freedom of the individual.

But we are faced with a different question here, even more serious than the first. It seems as though this law regresses humanity instead of promoting it. This is because while most of humanity is undeveloped, and the developed ones are always a small minority, if you always determine according to the will of the collective, which are the undeveloped, and the reckless ones, the views and desires of the wise and the developed in society, which are always the minority, will never be heard taken and will not be taken into consideration. Thus, you seal off humanity's fate to regression, for it will not be able to make even a single step forward.

However, as is explained in the article, "The Peace," section, "Necessity to Practice Caution with the Laws of Nature," since we are ordered by Providence to lead a social life, we have become obligated to observe all the laws pertaining to the sustenance of society. And if we are somewhat negligent, nature will take its revenge in us, regardless of whether or not we understand the reasons for the laws.

And we can see that there is no other arrangement by which to live in society except following the law of "Taking after the collective," which sets every dispute and tribulation in society in order. Thus, this law is the only instrument that gives society sustainability. For this reason, it is considered one of the natural *Mitzvot* (commandments) of Providence, and we must accept it and guard it meticulously, regardless of our understanding.

This is similar to all the other *Mitzvot* in the Torah: all of them are nature's laws and His Providence, which come to us from Above downward. And I have already described ("The Essence of the Wisdom of Kabbalah," The Law or Root and Branch) how the whole of reality that we detect in the conduct of nature in this world is only because they are extended and taken from laws and conducts of Upper, Spiritual Worlds.

Now you can understand that the *Mitzvot* in the Torah are no more than laws and conducts set in Higher Worlds, which are the roots of all of nature's conducts in this world of ours. The laws of the Torah always match the laws of nature in this world as two drops in a pond. Thus, we have proven that the law, "Taking after the collective," is the law of Providence and nature.

A PATH OF TORAH AND A PATH OF PAIN

Yet, our question about the regression, which had emerged from this law, is as yet not settled by these words. Indeed, this is our concern—to find ways to mend that. But Providence, for itself, does not lose because of that, for it has enveloped humankind in two ways—the "Path of Torah," and the "Path of Pain"—in a way that guarantees humanity's continuous development and progress toward the goal without any reservations ("The Peace," Everything Is in Deposit). Indeed, obeying this law is a necessary commitment.

THE COLLECTIVE'S RIGHT TO EXPROPRIATE THE FREEDOM OF THE INDIVIDUAL

We must ask further: things are justified when matters revolve around issues between people. Then we can accept the law of "Taking after the collective," through the obligation of Providence, which instructs us to always look after the well-being and happiness of the friends. But the Torah obliges us to follow the law of "Taking after the collective" in disputes between man and God, as well, although these matters seem completely unrelated to the existence of society.

Therefore, the question still stands: how can we justify that law, which obligates us to accept the views of the majority, which is, as we have said, undeveloped, and to reject and annul the opinion of the developed, which are always a small minority?

But as we have shown ("The Essence of Religion and Its Purpose," Conscious Development and Unconscious Development), the Torah and the *Mitzvot* were given only to purify Israel, to develop in us the sense of recognition of evil, imprinted in us at birth, which is generally defined as our self-love, and to come to the pure good defined as the "love of others," which is the one and only passage to the love of God.

Accordingly, the precepts between man and God are considered tools that detach man from self-love, which is harmful for society. It is thus obvious that the topics of dispute regarding *Mitzvot* between man and God relate to the problem of society's sustainability. Thus, they, too, fall into the framework of "Taking after the collective."

Now we can understand the conduct of discriminating between *Halachah* (Jewish law) and *Agadah* (legends). This is because only in *Halachot* (plural for *Halachah*), does the law, "individual and collective, *Halachah* (law) as the collective," apply. It is not so in the

Agadah, since matters of *Agadah* stand above matters that concern the existence of society, for they speak precisely of the matter of people's conducts in matters concerning man and God, in that part that has neither direct relation nor consequences relating to the existence and the physical happiness of society.

Thus, there is no justification for the collective to annul the view of the individual and (Every man did that which was right in his own eyes?). But regarding *Halachot* that deal with observing the *Mitzvot* of the Torah, all of which fall under the supervision of society, since there cannot be any order except through the law, "Take after the collective."

Now we have come to a clear understanding of the sentence concerning the freedom of the individual. Indeed, there is a question: "Where did the collective take the right to expropriate the freedom of the individual and deny him of the most precious thing in life, freedom?" Seemingly, there is no more than brute force here.

But as we have clearly explained above, it is a natural law and the decree of Providence. And because Providence compels each of us to conduct a social life, it naturally follows that each person is obligated to secure the existence and well-being of society. And that cannot exist but through imposing the conduct of "Taking after the Collective," ignoring the opinion of the individual.

Thus, you evidently see that this is the origin of every right and justification that the collective has to expropriate the freedom of the individual against his will, and to place him under its authority. Therefore, it is understood that with regard to all those matters that do not concern the existence of the material life of the society, there is no justification for the collective to rob and abuse the freedom of the individual in any way. And if they do, they are deemed robbers and thieves who prefer brute force to any right and justice in the world, since here the obligation of the individual to obey the will of the collective does not apply.

IN SPIRITUAL LIFE – THE LAW,
"TAKE AFTER THE INDIVIDUAL"

It turns out that as far as spiritual life is concerned, there is no natural obligation on the individual to commit him to society. On the contrary, here applies a natural law over the collective, to subjugate itself to the individual. And it is clarified in the Article, "The Peace," that there are two ways by which Providence has enveloped and surrounded us, to bring us to the end: a Path of Pain, which develops us in this manner unconsciously, and a Path of Torah and wisdom, which consciously develops us in this manner without any agony or coercion.

And since the more developed in the generation is certainly the individual, it follows that when the public wants to relieve themselves of the terrible agony and assume conscious and voluntary development, which is the path of Torah, they have no choice but to subjugate themselves and their physical freedom to the discipline of the individual, and obey the orders and remedies that he will offer them.

Thus you see that in spiritual matters, the authority of the collective is overturned and the law of "Taking after the Individual" is applied, that is, the developed individual. For it is plain to see that the developed and the educated in every society are always a small minority. It follows that the success and spiritual well-being of society is bottled and sealed in the hands of the minority.

Therefore, the collective is obliged to meticulously guard all the views of the few, so they will not perish from the world. This is because they must know for certain, in complete confidence, that the truer and more developed views are never in the hands of the collective in authority, but rather in the hands of the weakest, that is, in the hands of the indistinguishable minority. This is because every wisdom and everything precious comes into the world in small quantities. Therefore, we are cautioned to preserve the views of all the individuals, due to the collective's inability to tell wrong from right among them.

CRITICISM BRINGS SUCCESS; LACK OF CRITICISM CAUSES DECADENCE

We must further add that reality presents to our eyes extreme oppositeness between physical things and the concepts and ideas regarding the above topic. For the matter of social unity, which can be the source of every joy and success, applies particularly among bodies and bodily matters in people, and the separation between them is the source of every calamity and misfortune.

But with concepts and ideas, it is the complete opposite: unity and lack of criticism is deemed the source of every failure and hindrance to all the progress and didactic fertilization. This is because drawing the right conclusions depends particularly on the multiplicity of disagreements and separation between opinions. The more contradictions there are between opinions and the more criticism there is, the more the knowledge and wisdom increase and matters become more suitable for examination and clarification.

The degeneration and failure of intelligence stem only from the lack of criticism and disagreement. Thus, evidently, the whole basis of physical success is the measure of unity of the society, and the basis for the success of intelligence and knowledge is the separation and disagreement among them.

It turns out that when humankind achieves its goal, with respect to the success of the bodies, by bringing them to the degree of complete love of others, all the bodies in the world will unite into a single body and a single heart, as written in the article, "The Peace." Only then will all the happiness intended for humanity become revealed in all its glory.

But against that, we must be watchful not to bring the views of people so close that disagreement and criticism might be terminated from among the wise and scholarly, for the love of the body naturally brings with it proximity of views. And should criticism and disagreement vanish, all progress in concepts and ideas will cease, too, and the source of knowledge in the world will dry out.

This is the proof of the obligation to caution with the freedom of the individual regarding concepts and ideas. For the whole development of the wisdom and knowledge is based on that freedom of the individual. Thus, we are cautioned to preserve it very carefully, so each and every form within us, which we call "individual," that is, the particular force of a single person, generally named the "will to receive."

ANCESTRAL HERITAGE

All the details of the pictures that this will to receive includes, which we have defined as the "source," or the First Reason, whose meaning includes all the tendencies and customs inherited from his ancestors, which we picture as a long chain of thousands of people who once were alive, and who stand one atop of the other. Each of them is an essential drop of his ancestors, and that drop brings each person all the spiritual possessions of his ancestors into his elongated brain, in a way that the individual before us has all the thousands of spiritual legacies from all the individuals represented in that chain, which are his ancestors.

Thus, just as the face of each and every person differs, so their views differ. There are no two people on earth whose opinions are identical, because each person has a great and sublime possession inherited from his ancestors, and which others have no shred of them.

Therefore, all those possessions are considered the individual's property, and society is cautioned to preserve its flavor and spirit so as to not be blurred by its environment. Rather, each individual should maintain the integrity of his inheritance. Then, the contradiction and oppositeness between them will remain forever, to forever secure the criticism and progress of the wisdom, which is humanity's advantage and its true eternal desire.

And after we have come to a certain measure of recognition in man's selfishness, which we have determined as a force and a "will to receive," being the essential point of the bare being, we have also learned thoroughly clear, from all sides, the original possession of each body, which we have defined as "ancestral heritage." This pertains to all the potential tendencies and qualities that have come into his "source" by inheritance, which is the first substance of every person, that is, the initial seed of his forefathers.

Now we have found a way to understand our sages' meaning in what they said, that by the reception of the Torah, they were liberated from the angel of death. However, we need further understanding concerning the selfishness and the above-mentioned ancestral heritage.

Two Discernments: A) Potential, B) Actual

First, we must understand that although this selfishness, which we have defined as the "will to receive," is the very essence of man, it cannot exist in reality even for a second. (This is because it is known that there is a discernment of "potential" and a discernment of "actual." And this thing, which we call "potential," is a conceptual thing, before it has manifested from potential into actual. It is determined only in the **thought**.) For what we call "potential," meaning before it emerges from potential to actual, exists only in our **thought**, meaning that only the **thought** can determine it.

But in fact, there cannot be any real force in the world that is dormant and inactive. This is because the force exists in reality only while it is revealed in action. By the same token, you cannot say about an infant that it is very strong when it cannot lift even the lightest weight, but you can say that you see in that infant that when it grows, it will manifest great strength.

However, we do say that that strength we find in man when he is grown was present in his organs and his body even when he was an infant, but that strength had been concealed and was not apparent. It is true that in our minds we could determine (the powers destined to manifest), since the mind asserts it. However, in the infant's actual body there is certainly no strength at all, since no strength manifests in the infant's actions.

So it is with appetite. This force will not appear in a man's body in the actual reality, when the organs cannot eat, meaning when he is satiated. But even when one is satiated, the force of appetite exists, but it is concealed in man's body. After some time, when the food had been digested, it reappears and manifests from potential to actual.

However, such a sentence (of determining a potential force that has not yet been revealed in actual fact) belongs to the conducts by which the thought perceives. But it does not exist in reality, since when satiated, we feel very clearly that the force of appetite is gone, and if you search for it, you will find it nowhere.

It turns out that we cannot display a potential as a subject that exists in and of itself, but only as a predicate. Thus, when an action occurs in reality, at that time the force manifests in the action.

Yet, we necessarily find two things here, in the perceiving process: a subject and a predicate, that is, potential and actual, such as the force of appetite, which is the subject, and the image of the dish, which is the predicate and the action. In reality, however, they come as one. It will never occur that the force of appetite will appear in a person without picturing the dish he wishes to eat. Thus, these are two halves of the same thing. The force of appetite must dress in the image of the thing being eaten. This is because disclosure occurs only by clothing in that image. You therefore see that the subject and the predicate are presented as two halves of the same thing. Their presence appears at once, and disappears at once.

Now we understand that the will to receive, which we presented as selfishness, does not mean that it exists so in a person, as a craving force that wishes to receive in the form of a passive predicate. Rather, this pertains to the subject, which dresses in the image of the things that merit reception. Such is the force of appetite, which dresses in the image of the thing that is worth eating, and whose operation appears in the form of the thing being eaten, and in which it clothes. We call that action, "desire," meaning the force of appetite, revealed in the action of the imagination.

And so it is with our topic—the general will to receive, which is the very essence of man. It appears and exists only through dressing in the shapes of objects that are likely to be received. For then it exists as the subject, and in no other way. We call that action, "life," meaning man's livelihood, which means that the force of the will to receive dresses and acts within the desired objects. And the measurement of revelation of that action is the measurement of his life, as we have explained in the act we call, "desire."

TWO CREATIONS: A) MAN, B) A LIVING SOUL

From the above, we can clearly understand the verse: "And the Lord God formed man of the dust of the ground, and breathed into his nostrils the breath of life; and man became a living (*Chayah*) soul (*Nefesh*)" (Genesis 2:7). Here we find two creations: man himself, and the living soul itself.

And the verse says that in the beginning, man was created as dust of the ground, a collection of molecules in which resides the essence of man, meaning his will to receive. That force, the will to receive, is present in every element of reality, as we have explained above. Also, all four types: still, vegetative, animate and speaking emerged from them. In that respect, man has no advantage over any part of creation, and this is the meaning of the verse in the words: "dust of the ground."

However, we have already seen that this force, called "will to receive," cannot exist without dressing and acting in a desired object, and this action is called, "life." And accordingly, we find that before man has arrived at the human forms of reception of pleasure, which differ from those of other animals, he is still considered a lifeless, dead person. This is because his will to receive has no place in which to dress and manifest his actions, which are the manifestations of life.

This is the meaning of the verse, "and breathed into his nostrils the breath of life," which is the general form of reception suitable for humans. The word, Nishmat, (breath) comes from the word, Samin, (placing) the ground for him, which is like "value" (and the origin of the word "breath" is understood from the verse (Job 33:4): "The spirit of God has made me, and the breath of the Almighty has given me life," and see the commentary of the MALBIM there). The word, "soul" (Neshama), has the same syntax structure as the words, "missing" (Nifkad), "accused" (Ne'esham), and "accused" (Ne'eshama— female term of Ne'esham).

And the meaning of the words, "and breathed into his nostrils" is that He instills a soul (Neshama) in his internality and an appreciation of life, which is the sum of the forms that are worthy of reception into his will to receive. Then, that force, the will to receive, enclosed in his molecules, has found a place in which to dress and act, meaning in those forms of reception that he had obtained from the Creator. And this action is called, "life," as we have explained above.

And the verse ends, "and man became a living soul." This means that since the will to receive has begun to act by the measures of those forms of reception, life instantly manifested in it and it "became a living soul." However, prior to the attainment of those forms of reception, although the force of the will to receive had been imprinted in him, it is still considered a lifeless body, since it has no place in which to appear and to manifest in action.

One Commandment

Serving people by God's commandment; the part of the Torah concerning relations between man and man; speech, thought, and action; unintentionally bringing contentment to one's Maker; prophetic truth in physical measurement; the necessity to keep the 613 commandments; the wisdom of truth; prophecy; prophetic success is speed; the smaller may succeed more than the greater; prophecy through the generations; the essence of prophetic success; a general force and a particular force.

"If he performs one *Mitzva* (commandment), he is happy, for he has sentenced himself and the whole world to a scale of merit."

There is no serving the Creator and keeping the *Mitzvot* (commandments) except in *Lishma* (for Her Name)—bringing contentment to One's Maker. Yet, our sages have already introduced the practice of engaging in Torah and *Mitzvot* even in *Lo Lishma* (not for Her Name), since "from *Lo Lishma* he will come to *Lishma*"... I say that the first, and only *Mitzva* (commandment) that guarantees the achievement of the aspiration to attain *Lishma*, is to resolve not to work for oneself, apart from the necessary works—to merely provide for one's sustenance. In the rest of the time, one will work for the public: save the oppressed, and every creature in the world that is in need of salvation and benefit.

SERVING PEOPLE BY GOD'S COMMANDMENT

There are two advantages to this *Mitzva*:

1. Everyone will understand that they are working because this work is approved and agreeable to all the people in the world.

2. This *Mitzva* may better qualify one to keep Torah and *Mitzvot Lishma*, since the preparation is part of the goal. This is so because by accustoming oneself to serving people, one benefits others and not oneself. Thus, one becomes gradually fit to keep the *Mitzvot* of the Creator with the required condition— benefitting the Creator and not oneself. Naturally, the intention should be to keep the *Mitzvot* of the Creator.

THE PART OF THE TORAH CONCERNING RELATIONS BETWEEN MAN AND MAN

There are two parts to the Torah: one concerns man and God; the other concerns man and man. And I call upon you to, at any rate, engage and assume that which concerns man and man, since thus you will also learn the part that concerns man and God.

SPEECH, THOUGHT, AND ACTION

Work, of any kind, should include thought, speech, and action.

We have already explained the "practical" part of the one *Mitzva*: one should agree to dedicate all of one's free time to benefit the people in the world. The aspect of "thought" is more essential in this *Mitzva* than in *Mitzvot* relating to man and God. This is because in *Mitzvot* between man and God, the "act" in itself testifies that the intention is to benefit one's Maker, as there is no other room for such an action but Him.

Yet, with what concerns man and man, they are justified in and of themselves, since human conscience necessitates them. However, if one performs them from this perspective, he has not done a thing. In others words, these actions will not bring him closer to the Creator and to actual work *Lishma*.

Thus, each person should think that one is doing all that only to bring contentment to one's Maker, and to resemble His ways: as He is merciful, I am merciful, and as He always imparts good, so do I. This image, coupled with good deeds, will bring one closer to the Creator in a way that will equalize one's form to spirituality and to *Kedusha* (holiness). In this manner, one becomes like a seal, fit to receive the true Higher Abundance.

The "speech" refers to the prayer in the mouth—during the work and in fixed times—for the Creator to turn one's heart from "reception to bestowal." Also, it is contemplating the Torah and matters that promote achieving it.

Unintentionally Bringing Contentment to One's Maker

It is hopeless to wait for a time when a solution is found for allowing one to begin the work of the Creator in *Lishma*. As in the past, so in the future—every servant of the Creator must begin the work in *Lo Lishma*, and from that achieve *Lishma*.

And the way to achieving this degree is not limited by time, but by its qualifiers, and by the measure of one's control over one's heart. Hence, many have fallen, and will fall, in the field of working *Lo Lishma*, and die without wisdom. Yet, their reward is nevertheless great, since one's mind cannot appreciate the true merit and value of bringing contentment to one's Maker. Even if one works not under this condition, since one is not worthy of another way, one still brings contentment to one's Maker. And this is called "unintentionally."

Prophetic Truth in Physical Measurement

Since it is an absolute certainty, the prophetic abundance must be received in those combinations of letters completely suitable for the spirit of beginners, that is, to benefit them and to be open to the self-interest of the generation. This is so because only then is it guaranteed that God's word is accepted by the generation in the form of *Lo Lishma*, since the Creator did not prepare them in any other way.

Hence, this is the sign of a true prophet: his prophecy is best suited for the physical success of his contemporaries, as it is written, "And what great nation is there, that hath statutes and ordinances so righteous as all this law, which I set before you this day?" It is so because the nearness of the physical success will confirm their truthfulness, that, in the end, it is indeed the inlet.

The Necessity to Keep the 613 Commandments

The 613 names, considered the Holy Names, concern Private Providence for all who approach the reception of the Godly Abundance. One must experience all these orders without missing even one. Hence, the complete crave them with their hearts and souls, to keep them down to their corporeal branches, as it is written, "in every place where I cause My name to be mentioned I will come unto thee and bless thee."

THE WISDOM OF TRUTH

Earlier sages chose a private way for themselves, and I chose a general way, since, in my view, it better suits the Godly matter to be clothed in eternal letter-combinations that will never change. I wish to say that with physical success, they will not change in any place and in any time. For this reason my words are limited.

Because of the above reason, I was compelled to express spirituality in a general manner. Yet, instead, I chose to explain all the details and spiritual combinations down to very small details, which have no other source and origin other than this collective, that is, the purity of Kabbalah. And since I clarify the spiritual details without clothing in corporeal combinations, it will do much good to the development of attainment. And this wisdom is called "the wisdom of truth."

PROPHECY

There cannot be mistakes or lies in prophecy, as how can there be a mistake in the Light of Truth that stems from the Creator? Rather, it is as certain as the rain and the snow that fall from the sky and do not return there until their mission is successfully accomplished. Yet, there is a difference in the receiver, in the earth: soil that has been prepared by stone-removal and by plowing is more suited to receive than unprepared soil. Everything depends on the preparation.

Also, there are certainly differences among the receiving prophets. One is not the same degree as the other. Greatness and smallness are measured by the preparation in that prophet: one in a lower degree, due to absence of superb preparation, will necessarily miss some inclination in the course of the Light that pours upon him, of which it could be said that the Light of prophecy does not suffer any mistakes. Yet, one's smallness causes him multiplication in letter-combinations, which is multiplication of hoses and vessels until he attains prophecy.

PROPHETIC SUCCESS IS SPEED

Although the truth in the prophecy ultimately appears in the desirable success, a prophet of a smaller degree still compels a longer way upon the people to whom he has been sent. Conversely, one of a greater degree, whose preparation is more complete, will suffer no deflection upon receiving one's prophecy from the Creator. Hence, he will not multiply the vessels and hoses, for which his prophecy will be clear, concise, and easily accepted by those to whom he has been sent.

THE SMALLER MAY SUCCEED MORE THAN THE GREATER

But besides the above words, it is possible for the smallest of prophets to succeed in his prophecy even more than the greatest prophet—concerning the above-mentioned speed—since he relies on revelations of prior prophets, who paved his way for him. Obviously, it also depends on the development of his listeners, since clear and concise words require a more developed generation, so they can understand him. And if these two additions join one of small degree, he can succeed far more than a great one.

PROPHECY THROUGH THE GENERATIONS

Although Moses received the Torah and the laws for all the generations, to such an extent that the prophet is not entitled to any innovations, his prophecy was only given for a time. This is supported by the verse, "A prophet will the Lord thy God raise up unto thee, from the midst of thee, of thy brethren, like unto me;

unto him ye shall hearken." If Moses' prophecy were enough for all eternity, why would the Creator erect any other prophets such as him? Clearly, his prophecy was effective only for its time. And when that time is through, the Creator sends another prophet to continue and complement His will.

Yet, the prophet is not permitted to renew or subtract anything, for this would mean that there were a deficiency in the prior prophet. Rather, the words of God are always perfect, as it is written, "I am the first, and I am the last," and his only task is to extend that same prophecy to those generations that are no longer worthy of receiving from the first.

And the last prophet is the Messiah, who completes them all. He, too, is certainly not permitted to add or subtract, but his success will be greater, since the whole generation will be fit to accept his words and be completed through him. This is so for two reasons: either because of their greatness, or because of his contemporaries, or because of both.

The Essence of Prophetic Success

The essence of prophetic success is to extend the Upper Light to the dwellers below. The one who brings it lowest is the most successful. Above and below are measured in spirit and in physical benefit, since the physical obtained by prophecy is the point that gives people footing, and it is known that the focal point in the work of God is the first footing.

A General Force and a Particular Force

Their uniqueness is the unity of the Creator and the *Shechina* (Divinity). A particular force is the prohibition on reception down to the lowest degree, and the general force is multiplication of bestowal to complete dedication with all of one's heart.

Body and Soul

Before I clarify this exalted matter, it is important for me to note that although all the readers seem to consider it impossible to clarify and bring such a matter closer to the human mind, except by relying on abstract, philosophical concepts, as is usually the case in such scrutinies, since the day I have discovered the wisdom of Kabbalah and dedicated myself to it, I have distanced myself from abstract philosophy and all its branches as the east from the west. Everything that I will write henceforth will be from a purely scientific perspective, in utter precision, and by means of simple recognition of practical, useful things.

Although I will mention their words below, it will be only to indicate the difference between what the human mind can conjure up and what can be understood using the concepts of the Torah and the prophecy, which are based on practical foundations (as I have shown in "The Essence of the Wisdom of Kabbalah").

I would also like to thoroughly clarify the terms "body" and "soul" as they truly are, since truth and sound mind are one and the same. This is because the truth is available for anyone, but only by the spirit of the Holy Torah and by removing all the distorted concepts that have taken root among the people. These are primarily taken from abstract methods from which the spirit of our Holy Torah is utterly removed.

57

Three Methods in the Concepts of Body and Soul

In general, we find that the methods that abound in the world concerning the concepts of body and soul are gathered into three methods:

1) The Method of Faith

The method of faith argues that all that exists is the spirit, or the soul. They believe that there are spiritual objects separated from one another by quality. They are called "souls of people," and they exist independently, prior to dressing in a human body. Afterwards, when the body dies, the death does not apply to it, since a spiritual object is a simple object. In their view, death is but a separation of the elements comprising the object.

This is possible with physical objects, comprised of several elements which death disintegrates. But the spiritual soul, which is an utterly simple object, lacking any complexity, cannot be separated in any way, as this separation would annul its existence. Hence, the soul is eternal and exists forever.

The body, as they understand it, is like a clothing over this spiritual object. The spiritual soul clothes in it and uses it to manifest its forces: the good qualities and all kinds of concepts. Also, it provides the body with life and motion and guards it from harm. Thus, the body itself is lifeless, motionless, and contains nothing but dead matter, as we see it once the soul departs it—when it dies—and all the signs of life that we see in human bodies are but manifestations of the soul's powers.

2) The Method of Believers in Duality

Those who believe in duality think of the body as a complete creation, standing, living, and nourishing, and safekeeping its existence in all that is required. It does not need any assistance from any spiritual object.

Yet, the body is not considered man's essence. Man's primary essence is the perceiving soul, which is a spiritual object, as in the view of the supporters of the first method.

The difference between these two methods is only in the concept of the body. Following the extensive developments in physiology and psychology, they have found that Providence has provided for all of life's needs within the machine of the body itself. This, in their view, restricts the role of the soul's functionality within the body solely to concepts and virtues of the spiritual kind. Thus, while they believe in duality, in both methods together, they say that the soul is the reason for the body, meaning that the body is a result, extending from the soul.

3) The Method of the Deniers

The method of deniers of spirituality, who acknowledge only corporeality. Supporters of this method completely deny the existence of any kind of abstract spiritual object within the body. They have evidently proven that man's mind, too, is but a product of the body, and they depict the body as an electronic machine with wires that stretch from the body to the brain, and operate by encounters with external things.

Also, they send their sensations of pain or pleasure to the brain, and the brain instructs the organ what to do. Everything is run by wires and cords built for this task. They move the organ away from sources of pain and towards sources of pleasure. Thus, they clarify all of man's conclusions from life's events.

Also, what we feel as concepts and rationalities within our minds are but images of corporeal occurrences within the body. And man's pre-eminence over all animals is that our minds are developed to such an extent that all the body's events are depicted in our brains as images that we experience as concepts and rationalities.

Thus, the mind and all its deductions are but products that extend from the events of the body. In addition, there are proponents of the second method who completely agree with this method, but add the spiritual, eternal object to it, called "the soul that dresses within the machine of the body." This soul is **man's essence**, and the machine of the body is but its clothing. Thus, I have laid out in general terms all that human science has thus far contrived in the concepts of "body" and "soul."

THE SCIENTIFIC MEANING OF BODY AND SOUL ACCORDING TO OUR HOLY TORAH

Now I shall explain this exalted matter according to our Holy Torah, as our sages have explained it to us. I have already written in several places that there is not a single word of our sages, not even in the prophetic wisdom of Kabbalah, that relies on theoretical bases. This is so because it is a known fact that man is naturally doubtful, and each conclusion that the human mind deems certain, it deems uncertain after some time. Hence, one doubles the efforts of one's study and invents another inference and declares that as certain.

But if one is a genuine student, he will walk around this axis all of one's life, since yesterday's certainty has become today's uncertainty, and today's certainty become tomorrow's uncertainty.

Thus, it is impossible to determine any definite conclusions for more than a day.

Revealed and Concealed

Today's science has sufficiently understood that **there is no absolute certainty in reality**. Yet, our sages arrived at this conclusion several thousand years earlier. Hence, concerning religious matters, they have guided and forbidden us not only to refrain from drawing any conclusions based on theory, but even prohibited us from being assisted by such theories, even by way of negotiations.

Our sages divided the wisdom into two matters: revealed and concealed. The revealed part contains everything we know from our direct consciousness, as well as the concepts built upon practical experience, without any assistance from scrutiny, as our sages said, "a judge has only what his eyes see."

The concealed part contains all those concepts we had heard from trusted people or have acquired by ourselves through general understanding and perception of them. However, we cannot sufficiently approach it so as to criticize it with a healthy mind, with straightforward cognizance. And this is regarded as "concealed," where we were advised to accept matters with "simple faith." And with all that concerns religion, we have been strictly forbidden to even **gaze** at matters that could arouse us to scrutinize and **study them**.

Yet, these names, "revealed" and "concealed," are not permanent names, applying to a certain kind of knowledge, as the uneducated think. Rather, they apply only to the human **consciousness**. Thus, one refers to all those concepts one has already discovered and has come to know through actual experience as "revealed," and regards all the concepts that are yet to be recognized in this manner as "concealed."

Thus, throughout the generations, all people have these two divisions. The revealed part will be permitted for study and research, as it relies on a true basis, and the concealed part is forbidden for even a shred of scrutiny, since one has no real basis there.

PERMITTED AND FORBIDDEN IN USING HUMAN SCIENCE

Hence, we who follow in the footsteps of our sages are not permitted to use the human science, except with knowledge that has been proven by actual experiences, and of whose validity we have no doubt. Therefore, we cannot accept any religious principle from the above three methods, all the more so concerning the concepts of body and soul, which are the fundamental concepts and the subject of religion as a whole. We can only accept concepts of life sciences taken from experiments that no man can doubt.

Clearly, such a proof cannot be found in any spiritual matter, but only in physical matters, set up for perception by the senses. Hence, we are permitted to use the third method, to an extent. It engages only in **matters of the body**, in all those deductions that have been proven by experiments, and which no one doubts. The rest of the concepts, which combine the **reason** of their method and other methods, are forbidden to us. One who uses them breaches, "Turn you not unto the idols."

Yet, this third method is foreign and loathsome to the human spirit. There is hardly any truly educated person who is able to accept it. This is so because according to them, man's humane form has been erased and vanished. Man has been made into a machine that walks and works by other forces. According to them, man has no free choice whatsoever, but is rather pushed by nature's forces, and all his actions are compulsory. Hence, man has no reward or punishment, since no judgment, punishment, or reward apply to one who has no freedom of will.

Such a thing is utterly unthinkable, and not only for the religious, who believe in reward and punishment, since believing in His Providence, that all of nature's forces are guided by Him, assures them that everything has a good and desirable cause. Yet, this method is even stranger in the eyes of the nonreligious, who believe that everyone is given to the hands of a blind, mindless, and aimless nature. These intelligent ones are like toys in its hands, led astray, and who knows where? Hence, this method has become despised and unaccepted in the world.

But you should know that the method of those who conceive duality came only to correct this above-mentioned wrong. For this reason, they have decided that the body, which is but a machine according to the third method, is not at all the real human. Man's real essence is something altogether different—invisible and imperceptible to the senses. It is a spiritual entity, clothed and hidden within the body. This is man's "self," the "I." The body and everything within it are considered possessions of that eternal and spiritual I, as they have written.

Yet, by their own admission, this method is lame, since they cannot explain how a spiritual entity, being the soul or the self, can move the body or decide anything concerning it. This is because following the philosophical precision itself, the spiritual has no contact whatsoever with the physical. It has absolutely no impact on it, as they have written themselves.

THE ACCUSATION AGAINST THE RAMBAM (MAIMONIDES)

Yet, even without this question, their method would have been forbidden among Israel, as we have explained above. It is important to know that the whole accusation of Rambam by Israel's sages and the harsh judgment to burn his books were not because they had any doubt of the righteousness and piousness of the Rambam himself. Rather, it was only because he used philosophy and metaphysics, which were at their peak at the time, as assistance in his books. The Rambam wished to save them from it, yet the sages did not agree with him.

Needless to say, today our generation has already recognized that metaphysical philosophy contains no real content upon which it is worthwhile to spend one's time. Hence, it is certainly forbidden for anyone to take any spices from their words.

Peace in the World

"**M**ercy and truth are met together; righteousness and peace have kissed each other. Truth springeth out of the earth; and righteousness hath looked down from heaven. Yea, the Lord will give that which is good; and our land shall yield her produce."

~*Psalms* 85

EVERYTHING IS EVALUATED NOT BY ITS APPEARANCE AT A GIVEN MOMENT, BUT ACCORDING TO ITS MEASURE OF DEVELOPMENT.

Everything in reality, good and bad, and even the most harmful in the world, has a right to exist and should not be eradicated from the world and destroyed. We must only mend and reform it because any observation of the work of Creation is enough to teach us about the greatness and perfection of its Operator and Creator. Therefore, we must understand and be very careful when casting a flaw in any item of Creation, saying it is redundant and superfluous, as that would be slander about its Operator.

It is common knowledge that the Creator did not complete Creation when He created it. And we can see in every corner of reality, in the general and in the particular, that it abides by laws of gradual development, from absence to completion of growth. For this reason, when the fruit tastes bitter at the beginning of its growth, it is not considered a flaw in the fruit, since we all know the reason: fruit has not yet completed its development.

And so it is in every element of reality: when some element appears bad and harmful to us, it is but a self-testimony of that element; that it is still in the transition phase—in the process of its development. Hence, we cannot decide that it is bad and it is not wise for us to cast a flaw in it.

THE WEAKNESS OF "WORLD REFORMERS"

This is the key to understand the weakness of world-reformers throughout the generations. They regarded man as a machine that is not operating properly and needs mending, meaning to remove the corrupted parts and replace them with good ones.

And that is the tendency of all world reformers—to eradicate any harmful and bad in the human species... and it is true that if the Creator had not stood against them, they would certainly have by now cleansed man entirely, living only the good and useful.

But because the Creator meticulously watches over all the elements in His Creation, not letting anyone destroy a single thing in His Domain but only reform it and make it useful and good, all the reformers of the above-mentioned kind will vanish from the face of the earth, and evil inclinations will not vanish. They live on and count the degrees that they must still traverse until they complete their ripening.

At that time, the bad attributes themselves will turn to good and useful ones, as the Creator had initially perceived them to be, like the fruit on the tree that sits and waits and counts the days and months it must still wait before the completion of its ripeness, at which time its taste and sweetness will become evident to any person.

Rewarded—I Will Hasten It, Not Rewarded—in Its Time

We must know that the above-mentioned law of development, which is spread over the whole of reality, is guaranteed to return all evil to good and useful acts through the power of the Government of Heaven Above, meaning without asking permission from the people who inhabit the earth. However, the Creator placed knowledge and authority in the hands of man and permitted him to accept the above-mentioned law of development under his own authority and government, and handed him the ability to hasten the process of development as he wishes, freely and completely independent of the boundaries of time.

It turns out that there are two authorities here, acting in the above-mentioned conduct of development: the one is the authority of Heaven, which is sure to turn anything harmful and evil to good and useful, but that will be in due time, in its own way, in a floundering manner and after a long time. And then there is the authority of the earth. And when the "evolving object" is a living being, it suffers horrendous torments while under the "press of development," a press that carves its way ruthlessly.

The "authority of the earth," however, is comprised of people who have taken this above-mentioned law of development under their own government and can free themselves entirely from the chains of time, and who greatly accelerate time, the completion of the ripeness and correction of the object, which is the end of its development.

Such are the words that our sages said (*Sanhedrin* 98) about the complete redemption and complete correction of Israel. And thus they clarified the verse "I the Lord will hasten it in its time" (Isaiah 60:22): Rewarded—I will hasten it, not rewarded—in its time.

Thus, if Israel are rewarded and take the law of development that their bad attributes must go through in order to invert them into good ones, they will bring it under their own government. In other words, they will set their minds and hearts to correct all the bad attributes in them and turn them into good ones by themselves. Then, "I will hasten it," meaning they will be completely freed from the chains of time. And from now on, this end depends on their own will, meaning only by the greatness of the deed and the mindfulness. Thus, they hasten the end.

But if they are not rewarded with developing their bad attributes under their own authority, but leave it under the Authority of Heaven, they, too, are certain to attain the end of their redemption and the end of their correction. This is because there is complete certainty in the Government of Heaven, which operates by the law of gradual development, degree by degree, until it turns any evil and harmful to good and useful, as the fruit on a tree. The end is guaranteed, but in its time, meaning it is completely connected and dependent on time.

According to that law of gradual development, one must go through many degrees, which tend to come heavily and very slowly and lengthily, and stretch over a very long time before one reaches the end. And because the objects we are discussing are evolving, sensing, living beings, they, too, must suffer great agony and pains in those states of development, since the compelling force, which exists in those degrees in order to raise man from a lower degree to a Higher One, is but a pushing force of pain and torment that has accumulated in the lower degree and that can no longer be tolerated. Because of that, we must leave that degree and rise to a Higher One. It is as our sages said, "The Creator places over them a king whose sentences are as harsh as Haman's, and Israel repent and reform."

Therefore, the end is certain to come to Israel by the above-mentioned law of gradual development, and it is called "in its time," meaning tied to the chains of time. And Israel's guaranteed end, by taking the development of their attributes under their own authority is called, "I will hasten it," meaning completely independent of time.

Good and Bad Are Evaluated by the Actions of the Individual toward Society

Before we examine the correction of evil in the human species, we must first determine the value of those abstract terms, "good" and "bad." When we define an act or an attribute as good or bad, we should clarify whom that attribute or act benefits.

To understand that, we must thoroughly know the proportional value between the individual and the collective, between the individual and the collective that the individual lives in and nourishes from, in both matter and in spirit.

Reality shows us that there is no right to exist for an isolated individual without a sufficient number of people around him to serve him and help him provide for his needs. Hence, a person is born to lead a social life to begin with. And each and every individual in society is like a wheel that is linked to several other wheels, placed in a machine. And this single wheel has no freedom of movement in and of itself, but continues with the motion of the rest of the wheels in a certain direction, to qualify the machine to perform its general role.

And if there is some breakdown in the wheel, the breakdown is not evaluated relating to the wheel itself, but according to its service and role with respect to the whole machine.

And in our subject, the benefit of each and every person within his collective is evaluated not according to his own goodness, but according to his service to the public. And vice-versa, we appreciate the attribute of evil of each and every individual only according to the harm one inflicts upon the public in general, and not by one's own individual value.

These things are crystal clear both from the perspective of the truth in them, and from the perspective of the good in them. This is because what is found in the collective is only what is found in the individual. And the benefit of the collective is the benefit of each and every individual: who harms the collective takes his share in the harm, and who benefits the collective takes his share in the benefit, since individuals are part of the whole, and the whole is not worth in anyway more than the sum of its individuals.

It thus turns out that the collective and the individual are one and the same. And the individual is not harmed because of his enslavement to the collective, since the freedom of the collective and the freedom of the individual are one and the same, too. And as they share the good, they also share the freedom.

Thus, good attributes and bad attributes, good deeds and bad deeds are evaluated only according to the benefit of the public.

Of course, the above words apply if all the individuals perform their role toward the public to the fullest and receive no more than they deserve, and take no more than their friends' share. But if a part of the collective does not behave accordingly, it turns out that not only do they harm the collective but they are also harmed.

We should not discuss further something that is known to all, and the aforesaid is only to show the drawback, the place that needs correction, and that is that each and every individual will understand that his own benefit and the benefit of the collective are one and same thing. In that, the world will come to its full correction.

The Four Attributes, Mercy, Truth, Justice, and Peace, in the Individual and the Collective

Once we know full well the desired attribute of goodness, we should examine the things and the means at our disposal, in order to hasten that delight and happiness.

Four properties are provided for that purpose: mercy, truth, justice, and peace. Those attributes have been used by all world reformers thus far. It is more correct to say that it is with those four attributes that human development has advanced thus far through the government of Heaven, in a gradual path, until it brought humankind to its current state.

It has already been written that it would be better for us to take the law of development under our own hands and government, for then we will rid ourselves of any torment that the developmental history has in store for us from this day forth. Thus, we should scrutinize and examine those four properties in order to thoroughly understand what we have been given thus far and by them we will know what aid we should hope to get from them in the future.

Practical Difficulties in Determining the Truth

When we discuss good attributes, in theory, there is certainly no better attribute than the attribute of truth. This is because all the goodness that we have defined above in the relationship between the individual and the collective is when the individual gives and fully plays his part toward the collective, and also takes his share from the collective justly and honestly. All that is but the truth, but the drawback is that in fact, the collective does not accept this property at all. Thus, the practical difficulty in the above-mentioned truth is proven from itself: there is some drawback and a cause here that makes it unacceptable to the collective. And we must examine what is that drawback.

When you closely examine the above-mentioned truth from the perspective of its practical feasibility, you will necessarily find it vague and complicated, and it is impossible for the human eye to scrutinize it. That is, truth necessitates us to equalize all the individuals in the collective, to receive their share according to their labor, no more and no less. And this is the one true basis, which cannot be doubted, for it is certain that anyone who wishes to enjoy the labor of his friend, his acts are against the above-mentioned reason and clear truth.

But how do we think that we can scrutinize that truth in a way that it is acceptable to the collective? For example, if we evaluate something according to the apparent labor, meaning according to the number of hours, and we compel each and everyone to work an equal number of hours, we will still not discover the attribute of truth at all.

Moreover, there is an evident lie here for two reasons: The first is the physical side and the second is the mental side of the worker.

That is because by nature, the power to work is not equal with each and every person. One person in the society labors in one hour of work, due to his weakness, much more than his friend who works two hours or more.

And there is also a psychological matter here, because he who is very lazy by nature exhausts himself in one hour more than his friend in two hours or more. And according to the perspective of the evident truth, we should not compel one part of society to labor more than the other part for the fulfillment of the needs of their lives. In fact, the naturally strong and nimble in society benefit from the labor of others and exploit them maliciously against the attribute of truth, because they labor very little compared to the weak and the lazy in society.

And if we also consider the natural law, "Taking after the majority," then such a truth that takes the number of hours of apparent work as a basis is completely unfeasible, since the weak and the lazy are always the vast majority in society, and they will not allow the nimble and strong minority to exploit their strength and labor. Thus, you see that the above-mentioned basis, which is the labor of the individual on the condition of the evident truth, and with it the majority in the society, is completely unfeasible, since it cannot be examined and evaluated in any way.

Thus you find that the attribute of truth has no practical ability to organize the path of the individual and the path of the collective in an absolute and satisfactory manner. Also, it is completely insufficient for organizing life at the end of the correction of the world.

Furthermore, there are even greater difficulties here because there is no clearer truth than nature itself. And it is natural that each and every individual feels himself in the world of the Creator, as a sole ruler, that all the others were created only to ease and improve his life, without him feeling any obligation whatsoever to give anything in return.

And in simple words we shall say, that the nature of each and every person is to exploit the lives of all other people in the world for his own benefit. And all that he gives to another is only out of necessity; and even then there is exploitation of others in it, but it is done cunningly, so that his friend will not notice it and concede willingly.

The reason for it is that the nature of every branch is close to its root. And because man's soul extends from the Creator, who is One and Unique, and everything is His, hence, so man, who extends from Him, feels that all the people in the world should be under his own government and for his own private use. And this is an unbreakable law. The only difference is in people's choices: One chooses to exploit people by attaining lower desires, and one by attaining government, while the third by attaining respect. Furthermore, if one could do it without much effort, he would agree to exploit the world with all three together—wealth, government and respect. However, he is forced to choose according to his possibilities and capabilities.

This law can be called "the law of singularity in man's heart." No person escapes it, and each and every one takes his share in that law: the great according to his size, and the small according to his size.

Thus, the above law of singularity in the nature of every person is neither condemned nor praised, as it is a natural reality and has a right to exist like all parts of reality. And there is no hope to eradicate it from the world or even blur its form a little, just as there is no hope to eradicate the entire human species from the face of the earth. Therefore, we will not be lying at all if we said about this law that it is the absolute truth.

And since it is undoubtedly so, how can we even try to ease one's mind by promising him equality with all the people in the collective? For nothing is further from human nature than that, while one's sole inclination is to soar higher, above the whole collective.

Thus we have thoroughly clarified that there is no real possibility to bring good and joyful conducts to the life of the individual and the lives of the collective by following the attribute of truth in a way that it will ease the mind of each and every individual, so that he may completely agree with it, as it should be at the end of correction.

IN THE ABSENCE OF THE ABILITY TO ESTABLISH THE ATTRIBUTE OF TRUTH, THEY TRIED TO ESTABLISH THE NOBLE ATTRIBUTES

Now let us turn to the remaining three attributes: mercy, justice, and peace. It seems that to begin with, they were created only to be used as support for the weak attribute of truth in our world. And here, developmental history began to climb its slow and straggler degrees in its progress toward organizing the lives of the collective.

In theory, everyone willingly agreed and took it upon themselves to not deviate in any way from the truth. But in fact, they conducted themselves completely opposite from the truth. And since then, it has been the fate of truth to always be in the hands of the most deceitful and never in the hands of the weak and the righteous, so they could even be somewhat assisted by the attribute of truth.

When they could not establish the attribute of truth in the life of the collective, the exploited and the weak increased within society and from here emerged the attributes of mercy and justice and enacted their actions in the conduct of society, because the existence of the whole society compelled the successful among them to support the weak, so as to not harm the society in general. Therefore, they behaved with them indulgently, meaning mercifully and with charity.

But it is only natural that under such conditions the weak and the exploited proliferate, until there are enough of them to protest against the successful and start quarrels and fights. And from here emerged the attribute of "peace" in the world. Thus, all those attributes—mercy, charity, and peace—emerged and were born from the weakness of truth.

This is what caused society to divide into sects. Some adopted the attributes of mercy and charity, giving of their own possessions to others, and some adopted the attribute of truth, meaning "What's mine is mine and what's yours is yours."

In simpler words, we can divide the two sects into "constructors" and "destructors." Constructors are those who want construction, the benefit of the collective, for which they are often willing to give of their own possessions to others. But those who are naturally prone to destruction and profligacy were more comfortable clinging to the attribute of truth, meaning, "What's mine is mine and what's yours is yours," for their own gain, and would never want to give up anything of their own to others without taking into consideration jeopardizing the well-being of the collective, for as by nature they are destructors.

HOPES FOR PEACE

Once those conditions brought society a great deal of strife and risked the well-being of society, the "peacemakers" appeared in society. They have assumed control and power and renewed the social life based on new conditions, which they considered true, to suffice for the peaceful existence of society.

Yet, the majority of those peacemakers, which spring up after every dispute, naturally come from among the destructors, meaning from the seekers of truth, by way of "What's mine is mine and what's yours is yours." This is because they are the powerful and courageous ones in society, called "heroes," for they are always willing to renounce their own lives and the lives of the whole collective, if the collective disagrees with their view.

But the constructors in society, who are the men of mercy and charity, who care for their own lives and for the life of the collective, refuse to risk themselves or the public in order to impose their opinion on the collective. Hence, they are always on the weak side in society, called "the faint-hearted" and "the coward."

It is hence obvious that the hand of the brave profligates will always be on top, and it is natural that the peacemakers will come from among the destructors and not from the constructors.

Thus we see how the hope for peace, which our generation so yearns for, is futile both from the perspective of the subject and the perspective of the predicate.

For the **subjects**, who are the peace-makers of our time and in any generation, meaning those who have the power to make peace in the world, are forever made of the human substance we call "destructors," for they are seekers of truth, meaning to establish the world on the attribute of "What's mine is mine and what's yours is yours."

It is natural that those people defend their opinions firmly, to the point of risking their own lives and the life of the entire collective. And that is what gives them the power to always prevail over the human substance called, "constructors," the seekers of mercy and charity, who are willing to give up of their own for the good of others, in order to save the world, because they are the faint-hearted and the coward.

It turns out that seeking truth and the destruction of the world are one and the same, and the desire for mercy and the construction of the world are one and the same, too. Therefore, we should not hope from the destructors to establish the peace.

And it is hopeless to hope for peace from the predicate, meaning by the conditions of peace itself. This is so because the proper conditions for the well-being of the individual and the well-being of the collective, according to the criterion of truth that these peacemakers so desire, have not yet been established. And it is a must that there will always be a large minority in society who are unsatisfied by the conditions offered to them, as we have shown the weakness of the truth above. This minority will therefore always remain a ready and willing fuel for the new quarrelsome people and the new peacemakers that will always follow.

The Well-Being of a Certain Collective and the Well-Being of the Whole World

Do not be surprised if I mix together the well-being of a particular collective with the well-being of the whole world, because indeed, we have already come to such a degree that the whole world is considered one collective and one society. Meaning, because each person in the world draws his life's marrow and his livelihood from all the people in the world, he is coerced to serve and care for the well-being of the whole world.

We have proven above that the total subordination of the individual to the collective is like a small wheel in a machine. He draws his life and his happiness from that collective, and therefore the well-being of the collective and his own well-being are one and the same, and vice-versa. Therefore, to the extent that a person is enslaved to himself, he necessarily becomes enslaved to the collective, as we have spoken at length above.

And what is the extent of that collective? That is determined by the perimeter of the drawing of the individual from them. For example, in historic times, that perimeter was only the perimeter of one family, meaning the individual needed aid only from his own family members. At that time, he had to be subordinated only to his own family.

In later times, families gathered into towns and counties, and the individual became enslaved to his town. Later, when the towns and countries were joined into states, the individual was supported by all his countrymen for the happiness of his life. Thus, he became enslaved to all the people in the country. Therefore, in our generation, when each person is aided for his happiness by all the countries in the world, it is necessary that to that extent, the individual becomes enslaved to the whole world, like a wheel in a machine.

Therefore, the possibility of making good, happy, and peaceful conducts in one state is inconceivable when it is not so in all the countries in the world, and vice versa. In our time, the countries are all linked in the satisfaction of their needs of life, as individuals were in their families in earlier times. Therefore, we can no longer speak or deal with just conducts that promise the well-being of one country or one nation, but only the well-being of the whole world because the benefit or harm of each and every person in the world depends and is measured by the benefit of all the people in the whole world.

And although this is, in fact, known and felt, still the people in the world have not yet grasped it properly. And why? Because such is the conduct of the development in nature, that the act comes before the understanding, and only actions will prove and push humanity forward.

IN PRACTICAL LIFE, THE FOUR ATTRIBUTES CONTRADICT ONE ANOTHER

If the above practical difficulties, which disturb us helpless people on our way, are not enough, we have in addition a further mix-up and great battle of the psychological predispositions, meaning the attributes themselves within each and everyone of us individually, which are unique and contradictory to one another. For the four above attributes, mercy, truth, justice, and peace, which were divided in the nature of people, whether by development or by rearing, are in and of themselves contradictory to one another. If we take, for example, the attribute of mercy in its abstract form, we find that its government contradicts all other attributes, meaning that by the laws of the rule of mercy, there is no place for the appearance of the other attributes in our world.

What is the attribute of mercy? Our sages defined it, "What's mine is yours and what's yours is yours"—*Hasid*.[1] And if all the people in the world were to behave by this quality, it would cancel all the glory of the attribute of truth and judgment, because if each and every one were naturally willing to give everything he had to others, and take nothing from another, then the whole interest in lying to one another would disappear. Also, it would be irrelevant to discuss the quality of truth, since truth and falsehood are relative to one another. If there were no falsehood in the world, there would be no concept of truth. Needless to say, all the other attributes, which came only to strengthen the attribute of truth because of its weakness, would be cancelled.

Truth is defined in the words: "What's mine is mine, and what's yours is yours." That contradicts the attribute of mercy and cannot altogether tolerate it, since in truth it is unjust to labor and strain for another, because besides failing his friend and accustoming him to exploit others, truth dictates that every person should treasure his own assets for a time of need, so he will not have to be a burden on his fellow man.

Moreover, there is not a person without relatives and heirs that, in fact, should come before others, because so nature dictates that he who gives his property to others lies to his relatives and natural heirs by not leaving them anything.

And peace also contradicts justice because to make peace in the public, there must be conditions that by content promise the nimble and the smart, which invest their energy and wisdom, to become rich, and those who are negligent and naïve, to be poor. Hence, he who is more energetic takes his own share and the

---

1   Translator's Note: *Hasid* means one with the quality of *Hesed* (mercy).

share of his negligent friend and enjoys such a good life that there is not enough left for the negligent and naive to merely provide for their necessary livelihood. Hence, they remain completely bare and destitute in many ways.

It is certainly unjust to punish the negligent and the naive so harshly for no evil, for what is their sin and what is the crime of those wretched people, if Providence did not grant them agility and acumen that they should be punished with torments harsher than death?

Therefore, there is no justice whatsoever in the conditions of peace. Peace contradicts justice and justice contradicts peace, because if we order the division of property justly, meaning give to the negligent and naive a substantial portion of the part that the nimble and the energetic have, then these powerful and initiating people will certainly not rest until they overthrow the government that enslaves the great ones, the energetic ones, and exploits them in favor of the weak. Therefore there is no hope for the peace of the collective. Thus, justice contradicts peace.

THE ATTRIBUTE OF SINGULARITY IN THE EGOISM AFFECTS RUIN AND DESTRUCTION

Thus you see how our attributes collide and fight one another; and not only between sects, but within each person, the four attributes dominate him all at once or one at a time and fight within him until it is impossible for common sense to organize them and bring them to complete consent.

The truth is that the root of this whole disorder within us is no more than the above-mentioned attribute of singularity, which exists within each of us, whether more or less.

And although we have clarified that it comes from a sublime reason, that this attribute extends to us directly from the Creator, who is single in the world and the Root of all creations, still, out of the sensation of singularity, when it sits within our narrow egoism, it affects ruin and destruction until it became the source of all the ruins that were and will be in the world.

And indeed, there is not a single person in the world who is free from it, and all the differences are only in the way it is used— for the desires of the heart, for ruling, or for honor—and this is what separates people from one another.

But the equal side in all the people of the world is that each of us stands ready to abuse and exploit all the people for his own private benefit with every means possible, without taking into any consideration that he is going to build himself on the ruin of his friend. And it is inconsequential what allowance each of us gives himself, according to his chosen direction, since the desire is the root of the mind and not the mind the root of desire. In truth, the greater and more outstanding the person, precisely so is his attribute of singularity greater and outstanding.

USING THE NATURE OF SINGULARITY AS A SUBJECT OF EVOLUTION IN THE COLLECTIVE AND IN THE INDIVIDUAL

Now we shall penetrate into the understanding of the direct conditions that will finally be accepted by humanity at the time of the appearance of world peace, and learn how its conditions are good to bring a life of happiness to the individual and to the collective, and the willingness in humanity to want to finally burden themselves with those special conditions.

Let us return to the matter of singularity in the heart of every person, which stands to swallow the whole wide world for his own pleasure. Its root extends directly from the Unique One to the people, which are His branches. Here there is a question that demands an answer: "How can it be that such a corrupted form will appear in us so as to become the father of all harm and ruin in the world, and how from the Source of every construction extends the source of every destruction?" We cannot leave such a question unanswered.

Indeed, there are two sides to the coin of the above-mentioned singularity. If we examine it from its upper side, from the side of its equivalence with the Unique One, it works only in the form of bestowal upon others, for the Creator is all bestowal and has nothing of the form of reception, because He lacks nothing and needs to receive nothing from the creatures He has created. Therefore, the singularity that extends to us from Him must also act only in forms of bestowal to others, and to receive nothing for ourselves.

On the other side of that coin, meaning how it actually works in us, we find that it operates in the complete opposite direction, because it operates only in forms of receptions for oneself, such as the desire to be the only great and rich man in the whole world. Thus, the above two sides are as far apart from one another as the East from the West.

That gives us the solution to our question: "How is it possible that within the same singularity, which stems and comes to us from He Who is Unique in the world, Who is the Source of every construction, serves in us as the source of every destruction?" This has come to us because we use that precious tool in the opposite direction, which is self-reception. And I am not saying that the singularity in us will never act in us in a form of bestowal, because you cannot deny that amongst us are people whose singularity operates in them in the form of bestowal upon others, too, such as those who spend all their money for the common good, and those who dedicate all their efforts to the common good, etc.

But those two sides of the coin that I have described speak only of the two points of the development of Creation, which brings everything to completion, starting in absence, and gradually climbing the degrees of development, from one degree to the next Higher up, and from there to the Higher still, until it comes to the summit, which is its preordained measure of perfection. And there it will remain forever.

The order of development of those two points is, A) the starting point, the lowest degree, which is close to complete absence. It is described as the second side of the coin. B) The summit, where it rests and exists forever. And that is described in the first side of the coin.

But this era that we are in has already developed to a great extent and has already risen many degrees. It has already risen above its lowest phase, which is the above-mentioned second side, and has come significantly closer to the first side.

Therefore, there are already people among us who use their singularity in forms of bestowal upon others. But they are still few, as we are still in the midst of the path of development. When we come to the Highest point of the degrees, we will all be using our singularity only in a form of bestowal upon others, and there will never be any case of any person using it in a form of self-reception.

By those words, we find the opportunity to examine the conditions of life in the last generation—the time of world peace, when the whole of humanity achieves the level of the first side and will use their singularity only in the form of bestowal upon others, and not at all in the form of reception for self. And it is good to copy here the above-mentioned form of life so it will serve to us as a lesson and as a role model to settle our minds under the flood of the waves of our lives. Perhaps it is worthwhile and possible in our generation, too, to experiment in resembling this above form of life.

THE CONDITION OF LIFE
IN THE LAST GENERATION

First, everyone must thoroughly understand and explain to his surroundings that the well-being of society, which is the well-being of the state and the well-being of the world, are completely interdependent. As long as the laws of society are not satisfactory to each and every individual in the state, and leave a minority that is unsatisfied with the government of the state, this minority conspires under the government of the state and seeks to overthrow it.

And if its power is not sufficient to fight the government of the state face to face, it will want to overthrow it indirectly, such as to incite countries against each other and bring them to war, because it is natural that at war time there will be a lot more unsatisfied people with which they will have hope of achieving the critical mass to overthrow the government of the state and establish a new leadership that is convenient for them. Thus, peace of the individual is a direct cause for peace of the state.

Furthermore, if we take into consideration that that part in the state whose craftsmanship is war, which the state always has, and their every hope of success, such as the scholars of war and those who live by supplying the ammunition, that as far as the social quality is concerned, they are always a very significant minority, and if we add them to the unsatisfied minority from the current rules, at every given moment you have a vast amount of people who crave war and bloodshed.

Thus, peace of the world and peace of the state are interdependent. Hence, we necessarily find that even that part of the state which is currently satisfied with its life, which are the nimble and the clever, still have a lot to be concerned about for the safety of their lives, due to the tensions with those who strive to overthrow them. And if they understood the value of peace, they would be happy to adopt the conduct of living of the last generation, for "all that a man has will he give for his life."

Pain vs. Pleasure in Self-Reception.

Thus, when we examine and thoroughly grasp the above plan, we will see that the whole difficulty lies in changing our nature from a desire to receive for ourselves, to a desire to bestow upon others, since those two things deny one another. At first glance, the plan seems imaginary, as something that is above human nature. But when we delve deeply into it, we will find that the contradiction from reception for oneself to bestowal upon others is nothing but a psychological matter, because in fact we do bestow upon others without benefiting ourselves. This is so because although self-reception manifests itself in us in various ways, such as property, possessions for pleasure of the heart, the eye, the pallet, etc., all those are defined by one name, "pleasure." Thus, the very essence of reception for oneself that a person desires is nothing but the desire for pleasure.

And now, imagine that if we were to collect all the pleasures one feels during his seventy years of life and put it on one side, and collect all the pain and sorrow one feels on the other side, if we could see the outcome, we would prefer not to have been born at all. And if this is so, then what does one receive during one's life? If we assume that one obtains twenty percent of pleasure during his lifetime and eighty percent of pain, then if we put them one opposite the other, there would still remain sixty percent of suffering unrewarded.

But this is all a private calculation, as when one works for oneself. But in a global calculation, the individual produces more than he takes for his own pleasure and sustenance. Thus, if the direction were to change from self-reception to bestowal, the individual will enjoy the entire produce he produces without much pain.

The Love of God and the Love of Man

"Love thy friend as thyself." Rabbi Akiva says
this is a great rule in the Torah.

COLLECTIVE AND INDIVIDUAL

The above statement, although it is one of the most famous and cited sayings, it is still unexplained to everyone with all its vastness. That is because the word rule (or collective) indicates a sum of details that relates to the above rule, that each and every detail carries a part within it in a way that the gathering of all the details together creates that rule (or collective).

And if we say "a great rule in the Torah," it means that all the texts and the 612 *Mitzvot* are the sum-total of the details that relate to the verse of "Love thy friend as thyself." It is difficult to understand how such a statement can contain the sum-total of all the *Mitzvot* in the Torah? At most it can be the rule (the collective) of the part of the Torah and texts that relate to the *Mitzvot* between man and man. But how can you include the greater part of the Torah, which concerns work between man and God in the verse, "Love thy friend as thyself"?

That which You Hate, Do Not Do to Your Friend

If we can somehow reconcile the above text, here comes Hillel's statement to the foreigner who came before him and asked to be converted, as it says in the Gemarah, "Convert me so that you will teach me the entire Torah while I am standing on one leg." He told him "That which you hate, do not do to your friend." This is the entire Torah, and the rest are its interpretations, go and study. We evidently see that he told him that the entire Torah is the interpretation of the verse, "Love thy friend as thyself."

Now, according to the words of Hillel, the teacher of all the Kabbalists of his time, it is perfectly clear to us that the primary purpose of our holy Torah is to bring us to that sublime degree where we can observe this verse "Love thy friend as thyself", because it specifically says: "the rest are its interpretations, go and study." This means that they interpret for us how to come to that rule.

It is surprising that such a statement can be correct in most of the issues of the Torah, which concern man and God, when every beginner evidently knows that this is the heart of the Torah and not the interpretation of "Love thy friend as thyself."

Love Thy Friend as Thyself

We should examine further and understand the meaning of the verse, "Love thy friend as thyself." The literal meaning of it is to love your friend in the same amount that you love yourself. However, we see that the collective cannot keep up with it at all. If it had said love your friend as much as your friend loves you, there still would not be many people who could observe it completely, yet it would be acceptable.

But to love my friend as much as I love myself appears to be impossible. Even if there were but one person in the world except me, that would still be impossible, much less when the world is full of people. Moreover, if one loved everyone as much as one loves oneself, he would have no time for himself. But one must willingly satisfy one's own needs without neglect, for one loves oneself.

It is not so concerning the needs of the collective; for one has no strong motivation to stimulate one's desire to work for them. Even if one had a desire, could one still keep this statement literally? Would one's strength endure? If not, how can the Torah obligate us to do something that is not in any way feasible?

We should not consider that this statement is spoken by way of exaggeration, because we are cautioned by the saying: "Though shall not add to it nor subtract from it." All the interpreters agreed to interpret the text literally. Moreover they said that one must satisfy the needs of one's friend even in a place where one is himself in need. Even then we must satisfy the needs of our friend and leave ourselves needing.

The Tosfot interpret that anyone who buys a Hebrew slave, it is as though he buys a master for himself. And the Tosfot interpret that should one happen to have but one pillow, if one lies on it oneself, he does not keep, "For he is happy with thee." And if one does not lie on it and does not give it to one's slave, this is sodomite rule. It turns out that against his will one must give it to one's servant. It turns out that one has bought oneself a master.

One Mitzva (Commandment)

This raises several questions: According to the aforesaid, we all sin against the Torah. Furthermore we do not keep even the primary part of the Torah, the essence of it, because we keep the details but not the actual rule. It is written: "When you keep the will of the Creator, the poor are in others and not in you." Yet how is it possible that there will be poor when everyone keeps the rule, the desire of the Lord, and love their neighbor as themselves?

The issue of the Hebrew slave needs further study: The meaning of the text is that one must love one's slave as oneself even when referring to a stranger or an alien, who is not a Hebrew. And one should not excuse oneself because the rule for the stranger is as the rule for the Hebrew because "One law and one ordinance should be both for you and for the stranger that sojourneth with you." The word "stranger" also means a "partial proselyte," meaning one who does not accept the Torah, but only retires oneself from idolatry. It is written about such a person: "thou mayest give it onto the stranger that is within thy gates."

And this is the meaning of One Mitzva that the Tana speaks of when he says: "Performing one Mitzva sentences oneself and the entire world to a scale of merit." It is very difficult to understand what the entire world has to do with this. And we should not excuse ourselves that it is about when one is half righteous, half sinner.

One can see about oneself that one is half righteous, half sinner, but not that the entire world is such. Furthermore, the text should have stated "The whole of Israel"; but why does it say "the entire world"? Are we guarantors for the entire world? Do we add them into our account of good deeds?

We must understand that our sages spoke only of the practical part of the Torah, which brings the world and the Torah to the desired goal. Therefore, when they say One *Mitzva*, they certainly refer to a practical *Mitzva*. And this is certainly as Hillel says, meaning "Love thy friend as thyself." It is by this *Mitzva* alone that one attains the real goal, which is adhesion with the Creator. Thus you find that with this one *Mitzva* one keeps the entire goal and the purpose.

And now there is no question about the *Mitzvot* between man and God because the practical ones about them have the same purpose of cleansing the body, the last point of which is to love your friend as yourself. The immediate phase after that is adhesion.

And in that there is a general and a particular. We come from the particular to the general, because the general leads to the ultimate goal. Thus, it certainly makes no difference on which side to begin, in the particular or in the general, as long as we begin and do not stay neutral, until we reach our goal.

AND TO CLEAVE UNTO HIM

There still remains room to ask: "If the purpose of the Torah and the entire creation is but to raise the base humanity to become worthy of that wonderful sublimity, and to cleave unto Him, He should have created us with that sublimity to begin with, instead of troubling us with the labor that there is in creation and Torah and *Mitzvot*."

We could explain that by the words of our sages: "One who eats that which is not his is afraid to look at one's face." This means that anyone who feeds on the labor of others is afraid (ashamed) to look at his own form, for his form is inhuman.

Because no deficiency comes out of His wholeness, He has prepared for us this work, that we may enjoy the labor of our own hands. That is why He created creation in this base form. The work in Torah and *Mitzvot* lifts us from the baseness of creation, and through it we reach our sublimity by ourselves. Then we do not feel the delight and pleasure that comes to us from his generous hand, as a gift, but as owners of that pleasure.

However, we must still understand the source of the baseness that we feel upon receiving a present. Nature scientists know that the nature of every branch is to be close to its root. The branch also loves every conduct in the root. By the same principle, every thing that is not in the root, the branch too stays away from, cannot tolerate it and is harmed by it.

And because our root is the Creator, and He does not receive but gives, we feel sorrow and degradation upon every reception from another.

Now we understand the purpose of cleaving to Him. The sublimity of adhesion is only **the equivalence of the branch with its root**, and the whole matter of lowness is only **the remoteness from the root**. In other words, each creature whose way is corrected to bestow becomes sublime and capable of cleaving to Him. However, each creature whose way is reception and self-love, is degraded and removed far from the Creator.

As a remedy, we have been prepared with the Torah and *Mitzvot*. In the beginning we are to keep it *Lo Lishma*, meaning in order to be rewarded. This is the case during the period of *Katnut* (smallness), an educational phase. When one grows, one is taught to observe Torah and *Mitzvot Lishma*, meaning to bring contentment to one's Maker, and not for self-love.

Now we can understand the words of our sages, who asked, "Why should the Creator care if one slaughters through the throat or through the back of the neck? After all, the *Mitzvot* were only given to cleanse people with." But we still do not know what that cleansing is. With regards to the aforementioned, we know that, "a wild ass's colt is born a man." And we are completely immersed in the filth and lowness of self-reception and self-love, without any spark of love for one's fellow person and bestowal. In that state one is in the farthest point from the root.

When one grows and is educated through Torah and *Mitzvot*, defined only by the aim to bring contentment to one's Maker and not at all for self-love, one comes to the degree of bestowal to one's fellow person. One comes to that degree by the natural remedy in the study of Torah and *Mitzvot Lishma* that the Giver of the Torah knows, as our sages said, "I have created the evil inclination, I have created for it the Torah as a spice."

By that the creature develops in the degrees of the above sublimity until one loses any form of self-love and self-reception. In that state, one's every attribute is either to bestow, or to receive in order to bestow. Our sages said about that, "The *Mitzvot* were only given in order to cleanse people with," and then one cleaves to one's root, as it says, "and to cleave unto Him."

Two Parts to the Torah: Between Man and God and Between Man and Man

Even if we see that there are two parts to the Torah: The first – *Mitzvot* between man and God, and the second - *Mitzvot* between man and man, they are both one and the same thing. This means that the actual purpose of them and the desired goal are one, namely *Lishma*.

It makes no difference if one works for one's friend or for the Creator. That is because it is carved in us by the nature of creation that anything that comes from the outside appears empty and unreal.

Because of that we are compelled to begin with *Lo Lishma*. Rambam says, "Our sages said: 'One should always study the Torah, and even *Lo Lishma*, because from *Lo Lishma* one comes to *Lishma*.'" Therefore when teaching the young, the women and the illiterate, they are taught to work out of fear and in order to be rewarded until they accumulate knowledge and gain wisdom. Then they are told that secret little by little and they are accustomed to that matter with ease until they attain and know Him and serve Him with love."

Thus, when one completes one's work in love and bestowal for one's fellow person and comes to the highest point, one also completes one's love and bestowal for the Creator. In that state there is no difference between the two, for anything that is outside one's body, meaning one's self-interest is judged equally—either to bestow upon one's friend or bestow contentment upon one's Maker.

This is what Hillel Hanasi assumed, that "Love thy friend as thyself" is the ultimate goal in the practice. That is because it is the clearest form to mankind.

We should not be mistaken with deeds, for they are set before ones eyes. We know that if we place the needs of our friends before our own, this is the quality of bestowal. For that reason Hillel does not define the goal as "And you shall love the Lord your God with all your heart and with all your soul and with all your might," because they are indeed one and the same thing. It is so because one should also love one's friend with all his heart and with all his soul and with all his might, because that is the meaning of the words "as thyself." After all, one certainly loves oneself with all one's heart and soul and might, but with regards to the Creator, one may deceive oneself; and with one's friend it is always spread out before his eyes.

Why Was the Torah Not Given to the Patriarchs?

That answers the first three questions. But there still remains the question how is it possible to keep it, for it is seemingly impossible. You should know that that is why the Torah was not given to the Patriarchs, but to their children's children, who were a complete nation, consisting of 600,000 men from 20 years of age and on. They received it after having been asked if each and every one of them were willing to take upon himself this work and this sublime goal.

After each and every one said, "We shall do and we shall hear," it became possible. That is because undoubtedly, if 600,000 men have no other interest in life but to stand guard and see that no need is left unsatisfied in their friends, and they even do it lovingly, with all their soul and all their might, there is absolutely no doubt that there will not be a need in any person in the nation to care for his own sustenance. That is because he will have 600,000 loving and loyal people making sure not a single need is left unsatisfied.

Thus we answer the question why was the Torah not given to our holy patriarchs. That is because in a small group of people the Torah cannot be observed. It is impossible to begin the work of *Lishma*, as it is described above. Because of that the Torah was not given to them.

All of Israel Are Responsible for One Another

In light of the above we can understand a perplexing saying by our sages who said, "All of Israel are responsible for one another." Furthermore, Rabbi Elazar, the son of Rabbi Shimon adds that, "The world is judged by the majority."

It follows that we are also responsible for all the nations of the world. I wonder; this seems to be something that the mind cannot tolerate. How can one be responsible for the sins of another whom he does not know? It is said specifically that, "The fathers shall not be put to death for the children, neither shall the children be put to death for the fathers; every man shall be put to death for his own sin."

Now we can understand the meaning of the words in utter simplicity. It is clearly impossible to keep the Torah and *Mitzvot* if the entire nation does not participate.

It turns out that each and every person has become responsible for his friend. This means that those who are reckless make those who keep the Torah remain in their filth. They cannot be corrected and come to love bestowal upon one's fellow person without the participation of the reckless. Thus, if some among the nation are sinners, they make the rest of the nation suffer.

It is written in the Midrash, "Israel, one of them sins and all of them feel." Rabbi Shimon said about that: "It is like people who were seated in a boat. One of them took a drill and began to drill under his seat. His friends told him, 'What are you doing?' He replied, 'Why should you care? Am I not drilling under me?' They replied, 'The water is flooding the boat.'" As we've explained above, because the reckless are immersed in self-love, their acts create a wall of steel that detains those who keep the Torah from even beginning to keep the Torah and *Mitzvot*, as they should be kept.

Now we will clarify the words of Rabbi Elazar, son of Rabbi Shimon, who says, "Since the world is judged by the majority, and the individual is judged by the majority, if one performs one *Mitzva*, blessed be he, for he sentences himself and the entire world to a scale of merit. If he commits one sin, woe unto him for he sentences himself and the entire world to a scale of demerit. It is said, 'But one sinner destroyeth much good.'"

We see that Rabbi Elazar, son of Rabbi Shimon takes the issue of the *Arvut* (mutual responsibility) even further, for he says, "The world is judged by its majority." This is because he thinks it is not enough for one nation to receive the Torah and *Mitzvot*. Either he came to this opinion by observing reality, for we see that the end has not yet come, or he received it from his teachers.

The text also supports him, as it promises us that at the time of redemption, "the earth shall be full of the knowledge of the Lord," and also, "all nations shall flow onto Him," and many more verses. That is the reason he conditioned the *Arvut* in the participation of the entire world. It shows that an individual cannot come to the desired goal by observing Torah and *Mitzvot*, if not through the aid of all the people of the world.

Thus, each and every *Mitzva* that one performs affects the whole world. It is like a person who weighs beans on a scale. Just like each and every bean one puts on the scale induces the final desired decision, so each *Mitzva* that the individual performs before the whole earth is full of the knowledge develops the world in that direction.

It is said, "But one sinner destroyeth much good." It means that one's sinning reduces the weight on the scale, as though that person took back the beans he had put on the scale. By that one turns the world backwards.

WHY WAS THE TORAH GIVEN TO ISRAEL?

Now we can answer the question, "Why was the Torah given to the Israeli nation without the participation of all the nations of the world?" The truth is that the purpose of creation applies to the entire human race, none absent. However, because of the lowness of the nature of creation and its power over people, it was impossible for people to be able to understand, determine and agree to rise above it. They did not demonstrate the desire to relinquish self-love and come to equivalence of form, which is adhesion with His attributes, as our sages said, "As He is merciful, so you be merciful."

Thus, because of their ancestral merit Israel succeeded, and over 400 years they developed and became qualified and sentenced themselves to a scale of merit. Each and every member of the nation agreed to love his fellow man.

Being a small and single nation among seventy great nations, when there are a hundred gentiles or more for every one of Israel, when they had taken upon themselves to love their fellow person, the Torah was then given specifically to qualify the Israeli nation.

However, the Israeli nation was to be a "transition." This means that to the extent that Israel cleanse themselves by keeping the Torah, so they pass their power on to the rest of the nations. And when the rest of the nations also sentence themselves to a scale of merit, then the Messiah will be revealed. That is because the role of the Messiah is not only to qualify Israel to the ultimate goal of adhesion with Him, but to teach the ways of God to all the nations, as the verse says, "And all nations will flow onto Him."

Exile and Redemption

"And among these nations shalt though have no repose."

~Deuteronomy 28:85

"And that which cometh into your mind shall not be at all; in that you say we will be as the nations, as the families of the countries."

~Ezekiel 20:32

The Creator will evidently show us that Israel cannot exist in exile, and will find no rest as the rest of the nations that mingled among the nations and found rest, and assimilated in them, until no trace was left of them. Not so is the house of Israel. This nation will find no rest among the nations until it realizes the verse, "And from there you will seek the Lord your God and you will find Him for you will demand him with all your heart and all your soul" (Deuteronomy 4:29).

This can be examined by studying Providence and the verse which states about us, "The Torah is true and all its words are true, and woe to us as long as we doubt its truthfulness." And we say about all the rebuke that is happening to us that it is chance and blind fate. This has but one cure—to bring the troubles back on us to such an extent that we will see that they are not coincidental but steadfast Providence, intended for us in the Holy Torah.

And we should clarify this matter by the law of development itself: the nature of the steadfast Guidance that we have attained through the Holy Torah, as in the path of Torah in Providence (see "Two Ways"), a far more rapid development than the other nations has come to us. And because the members of the nation developed so, there was always the necessity to go forward and be extremely meticulous with all the *Mitzvot* of the Torah. And because they would not do it, but wished to include their narrow selfishness, meaning the *Lo Lishma*, this developed the ruin of the First Temple, since they wished to extol wealth and power above justice, as other nations.

But because the Torah prohibits it, they denied the Torah and the prophecy and adopted the manners of the neighbors so they could enjoy life as much as selfishness demanded of them. And because they did that, the powers of the nation disintegrated: some followed the kings and the selfish officers, and some followed the prophets. And that separation continued until the ruin.

In the Second Temple, it was even more conspicuous, since the beginning of the separation was publicly displayed by unvirtuous disciples, headed by Tzadok and Bytos. Their mutiny against our sages revolved primarily around the obligation of *Lishma*, as our sages said, "Wise men, be careful with your words." Because they did not want to retire from selfishness, they created communities of this corrupt kind and became a great sect called "Tzdokim," who were the rich and the officers, pursuing selfish desires unlike the path of Torah. And they fought the Prushim and brought the Roman kingdom's rule over Israel. They are the ones who would not make peace with the imperious, as our sages advised by the Torah, until the house was ruined and the glory of Israel was exiled.

THE DIFFERENCE BETWEEN A SECULAR IDEAL AND A RELIGIOUS IDEAL

A secular ideal stems from humanness and hence cannot raise itself above humanness. But a religious idea, which stems from the Creator, can raise itself above humanity. This is because the basis for a secular ideal is equalization and the price of **glorifying man**, and he acts to boast in the eyes of people. And although one is sometimes disgraced in the eyes of one's contemporaries, one still relies on other generations and it is still a precious thing for him, like a gem that fuels its owner although no one knows of it or cherishes it.

A religious idea, however, is based on **glory in the eyes of God**. Hence, he who follows a religious idea can raise himself above humanness.

And so it is among the nations of our exile. As long as we followed the path of Torah, we remained safe, for it is known to all the nations that we are a highly developed nation and they wanted our cooperation. They exploit us, each according to their own selfish desires. Yet we still had great power among the nations, for after all the exploitation, there still remained a handsome portion left for us, greater than for the civilians of the land.

But because people rebelled against the Torah in their aspiration to execute their selfish ploys, they lost life's purpose, meaning the work of God. And because the sublime goal was swapped for selfish goals of life's pleasures, anyone who attained fortune raised his own goal with glory and beauty. And where the religious man scattered his monetary surplus on charity, good deeds, building seminaries, and other such collective needs, the selfish ones scattered their surplus on the joys of life: food and drink, clothing and jewels, and equalized with the prominent in every nation.

By these words, I only mean to show that the Torah and the natural law of development go hand in hand in wondrous unity even with blind faith. Thus, the bad incidences in the exile, which we have much to tell of from the days of our exile, were all because we embezzled the Torah. And if we kept the commandments of the Torah, no harm would come to us.

CONGRUITY AND UNITY BETWEEN TORAH AND BLIND FAITH, AND THE DEVELOPMENT OF HUMAN CALCULATION

Hence, I hereby propose to the House of Israel to say to our troubles, "Enough!" and at the very least, make a human calculation regarding these adventures that they have inflicted us time and time again, and here in our country, as well. We wish to start our own policy, as we have no hope of clutching at the ground as a nation as long as we do not accept our holy Torah without any extenuations, to the last condition of the work *Lishma*, and not for oneself, with any residue of selfishness, as I have proven in the article "Matan Torah."

If we do not establish ourselves accordingly, then there are classes among us, and we will undoubtedly be pushed right and left as all nations are, and much more. This is because the nature of the developed is that they cannot be restrained, for any important notion that comes from an opinionated person will not bow its head before anything and knows no compromise. This is why our sages said, "Israel is the fiercest of the nations," as one whose mind is broader is most obstinate.

This is a psychological law. And if you do not understand me, go and study this lesson among the contemporary members of the nation: While we have only begun to build, time has already disclosed our fierceness and assertiveness of the mind, and that which one builds, the other ruins.

...This is known to all, but there is only one innovation in my words: They believe that in the end, the other side will understand the danger and will bow his head and accept their opinion. But I know that even if we tie them together in one basket, one will not surrender to the other even a little, and no danger will interrupt anyone from carrying out his ambition.

In a word: As long as we do not raise our goal above the corporeal life, we will have no corporeal revival because the spiritual and the corporeal in us cannot dwell in one basket, for we are the children of the idea. And even if we are immersed in forty-nine gates of materialism, we will still not give up the idea. Hence, it is the holy purpose of for His name that we need.

Thou Hast Hemmed Me in Behind and Before

World—Concealment / Surrender, Division, Mitigation
(Sweetening) / Remember and Keep were Said in One
Utterance / The Power of Speech / Blessing of the
Righteous / The End of a Matter Is Better than Its
Beginning / Two Opposites in the Same Subject / The
Quality of Jacob the Patriarch / Difference between One
who Serves the Creator and One who Does Not / The *Klipa*
of Ishmael and the *Klipa* of Esau

Thou hast hemmed me in behind and before, meaning the revelation and concealment of the face of the Creator. This is because indeed, "His kingdom ruleth over all," and everything will return to its root because there is no place vacant of him. But the difference is in present tense or future tense, because who connects the two worlds, discovers His clothing in the present: everything that is done is a clothing for the revelation of divinity.

And this is deemed the present tense, meaning that now, too, he comes out in royal clothes and evidently shows that the rider is not subordinate to the horse. But although it seemingly appears that the horse leads the rider, the truth is that the horse is provoked to any movement only by the sensation of the rider's bridle and headstall. And this is called "the construction of the stature of divinity," and it is also called "face-to-face."

But one who has not yet come to dedicate all his movements to the Creator alone, and the horse does not equalize its movements to the rider's bridle and headstall, but appears to do the opposite, and the handmaid appears to rule the mistress, this is called "behind." Hence, you should not think that you are drawing away from holiness, for "that which cometh into your mind shall not be at all."

Thus says the Lord: "Surely with a mighty hand," etc., "For he that is banished be not an outcast from him." And every wheel turns to come to holiness, its root. Therefore, although it seems that the horse leads the rider by its base desire, the truth is not so. It is the rider who leads the horse to his destination. However, it is not apparent in the present, but in the future. Hence, that way there is contact, as well, but it is back to back, meaning not by the will of the dresser or that of the dressee.

But those who follow His will discover for themselves the royal dresses in the present, connected face to face through the will of the dresser, for that is precisely His wish.

And this is the meaning of "Because thou hast not served the Lord thy God with joyfulness." For you will serve Him anyhow, but the difference is that this way is "in siege and in distress," meaning unwillingly, and the other way is by reason of the abundance of all things, meaning willingly.

It is also written in the Midrash: "The Creator gazes upon the deeds of the righteous and the deeds of the wicked, and He does not know which the Creator wants, whether the deeds of the righteous, etc. When He says, 'And God saw the light, that it was good; and God divided,' meaning in the deeds of the righteous."

This means that the Creator examines, meaning connects with all the deeds and conducts, and everything returns to its root. Hence, the question is, "Which way is more desirable? In that regard, the Midrash is assisted by the verse, "And God saw the light, that it was good," meaning disclosure, which is in the deeds of the righteous. This is our sages' meaning in saying, "Long and short, and short and long."

World—Concealment

This is the meaning of "In wisdom hast Thou made them all; the earth is full of Thy creatures." Everything is kept in the 32 paths of wisdom; hence, "the earth is full of Thy creatures and no place is vacant from it, for everything goes to its root. Now, however, it is concealed, and therefore called *Olam* (world), from the word *He'elem* (concealment).

And the Light that hides and clothes in the word is called "a point," considered a *Yod*. It is divided into the two *Heys*: the concealed world and the revealed world. And the whole of man's work is to reveal this point and extend it from the world to the world in the form of *Vav*, meaning the *Vav* between the *Heys*, to reveal to all the plentiful Light that extends from the Surrounding Light to the surrounded, meaning the two *Heys*, as in *Bina, Yesod, Malchut*.

Surrender, Division, Mitigation (Sweetening)

There are three discernments required of a man in the desirable path: surrender, division, mitigation (sweetening), meaning "Lights with deficient writing,"[2] since the Light of this world was created out of darkness, "as far as light excelleth darkness," and

---

2   Translator's Note: In Hebrew, words can be written with or without vowels. In the case of the word, "Light," it means writing with or without the letter Vav.

"What good is a candle during the day?", its light does not shine in the daytime. This is the meaning of the *Klipa* (peel) that precedes the fruit. For this reason, who becomes a partner to the Creator in the act of creation, brings the Light out of the darkness, meaning considers how lowly and base one is, compared to the sublime *Kedusha* (holiness), and how filthy are one's clothes. Through it, the Light becomes surrounded.

And in regards to the Creator's question, "to fear the Great and Terrible Name," he intensifies with great strength to subdue the evil within, so the evil servant and evil maid will surrender to the mistress, which dwells with them in the midst of their uncleanness, until he feels in his soul that the awakening for externality has expired and surrendered. At that time, he will be rewarded with "division," distinguishing between the Light and the darkness, and will not replace bad for good and good for bad. And should he replace, meaning awaken to a necessary inclination, it will be dedicated to the Creator only. This is considered "mitigation," the craving for the Creator, as in genuine love.

This discernment comes after he separates between the good and evil, between the Creator's sublimity and his own baseness, and keeps "So shalt thou put away the evil from the midst of thee" in himself, for he will be so very ashamed of its doers. Then he will be rewarded with mitigating the remains of his inclination, which cannot be rooted out, and elevate them to their genuine root.

REMEMBER AND KEEP WERE SAID IN ONE UTTERANCE

"Remember" and "Keep" were said in one utterance. What the mouth cannot say and the ear cannot hear, and the heart cannot think and contemplate, etc. We must understand why this was said in this way, and what does it mean to us?

It is written, "Man and beast Thou preservest, O Lord." Our sages said, "These are people who are of cunning mind and pretend to be as beasts." This means that the whole path of creation that the Creator created is regarded as two opposites in one subject, and all the combinations in the world were made in this way, and this is the whole of the act of creation.

THE POWER OF SPEECH

However, in the act of creation, the Creator revealed only one part of that discernment, as it is written, "By the word of the Lord were the heavens made," for He took fire and water and mixed them into a single subject. And the Creator imprinted the power of speech in man, so he would partner with Him in the act of creation, so he, too, would create worlds with his speech from this discernment, meaning two opposites in the same subject, for another innovation... world.

This is the way of the righteous, who cleave to the Creator: From all their utterances, the worlds were created according to the word of God, as well as the Operating force in the operated, since it had already imprinted in their mouths the twenty-two letters by which He had created the world. What I wish to say is that they contain that power.

And the reason why the doing does not end in this world by utterances alone is because of the descents of this world in materialization. For this reason, nothing appears by speech, but only by hands and legs. However, in truth, the Creator has imprinted sufficient strength in the speech by which to disclose all the actions, since the force of the Operator is in the operated. And we, too, express in our mouths those twenty-two letters.

Yet, the *Klipot* cover and weaken that force, and the Creator wished to cleanse Israel from the *Klipot*, hence He gave them Torah and *Mitzvot* by which they draw near to his *Kedusha* (holiness), and the *Shechina* (Divinity) speaks from their mouths in purity. At that time, they perform deeds with their speech.

BLESSING OF THE RIGHTEOUS

This is the meaning of the blessings of the righteous, who reveal by their utterances more than a simple man can reveal by hands and legs. This is because a simple man who wishes to do good to one's friend, give him much money with his hands, and makes him wealthy. Yet, he does not know if this will last very long.

But the whole one, who wishes to do good to his friend, gives him a blessing with his mouth—some short words of richness—and the act of enrichment instantaneously appears on one's friend, etc.

How is one rewarded with this? This happens through Torah and *Mitzvot*, meaning that by doing His will, one's form becomes similar to one's Maker. In truth, however, the whole issue of Torah and *Mitzvot* that connect to a person are also of the above-mentioned kind, meaning the two opposites in the same subject. This is the main thing that is desired, since the Creator created the world with the Torah, and the force of the Operator is in the operated. This is the essence of the knowledge, which we do not know: when these two opposites unite into a single *Guf* (body) in one's mind, he becomes desirable to his Maker and is considered "a whole man."

THE END OF A MATTER IS BETTER
THAN ITS BEGINNING

In essence, the giving of the Torah in this lowly world is an opposite thing, for the angels erred in it. This is the meaning of, "The end of a matter is better than its beginning." Interpretation: "The end of a matter" refers to the bottom of the degree, meaning at the creation of the world for all to see, when it requires no scrutiny. This is what the books call "first concepts," meaning if one does not eat, he will starve; if he touches fire, he will burn; and if he throws himself into the water, he will drown, etc. These things are understood by animals and beasts, too, since the animate mind will tell them this. This is why it is called "the end of a matter."

"The beginning of a matter" is the mind of the Torah, which is not attained even for the speaking, meaning to the populace, except to the seed of Joseph, God's select. In the world, good and evil are mixed. To distinguish between good and evil, the writing tells us that the primary way of the good is the "end of a matter," meaning to behave in a way that the lowly discuss, through what is attained to all the people, but to connect the mind of the Torah to it. This is so because this is the purpose of the opposites in the world, and the whole man must connect and unite in his mind in real unity. And this is called "good," as it is written, "The end of a matter," if it is well connected from its start, meaning the mind of the Torah and the animate mind actually connect into one.

TWO OPPOSITES IN THE SAME SUBJECT

This is the meaning of the words of our sages, "'Man and beast Thou preservest, O Lord,' these are people of a cunning mind, who pretend to be as beasts." We have explained above that these two opposites unite in them to one. Take for example what is written, "Without flour, there is no Torah; without Torah, there is no flour." In the first part, it is an animate mind—a mind attained by all. In the second part, it is the mind of the Torah, since how are the provision of flour and the power of the Torah connected? But from the Torah, we understand that the Creator never removes His Providence from the world for even a moment; hence, He benefits those who heed his will and hears their prayer.

Accordingly, those who have been rewarded with their labor being in the Torah certainly do not need to work as the populace, since they ask of the One who truly has, and He will give them, as it is written, "Since they are followers, their Torah is preserved and their work blessed." The Tana tells us, "Without flour," etc., meaning that the desirable way is to connect them, meaning to pretend to be as a beast, to know that without flour there is no Torah and hence to try one's hardest with what his corporeal mind teaches him to do in order to obtain flour and food for his body.

Indeed, the law of the Torah permits, for "He delighteth not in the strength of the horse; He taketh no pleasure in the legs of a man. The Lord taketh pleasure in them that fear Him, in those that wait for His mercy." Hence, why should He touch and strip a carcass in the market? To not need people, he prefers to engage in the Torah—to fear the Creator and to wait for His mercy, for "He taketh no pleasure in the legs of a man," etc. This is two opposites when they actually unite into one, in those who do as the beast and know that it is futile, and everything comes to him from the King's table. Such a man is called "whole."

This is the meaning of the verse, "Happy is the man that hath made the Lord his trust, and hath not turned unto the arrogant, nor unto such as fall away treacherously." He unites the two things: trusts in the Creator, strains with all his heart to provide food for his home, but knows that all his deeds and all his efforts are but arrogance and treachery, and he puts his trust in the Creator.

It is written, "For the rod of wickedness shall not rest upon the lot of the righteous." This means that although their acts are similar, etc. Why? The writing interprets, "that the righteous put not forth their hands unto iniquity," for they completely assume the burden of the kingdom of heaven and know that He is the one who gives you strength.

The reason for it is to see how far the faith of the righteous reaches. And although the Creator knows the thoughts, the deeds must still be clear to the righteous himself. This is because it is the nature of matter that it does not let the righteous believe in themselves until they evidently and actually see, and they are always afraid lest they will inflict sin and fall from their degree during the deed.

THE QUALITY OF JACOB THE PATRIARCH

Now we can understand what our sages said, that Jacob returned to the small tins. It is indeed a wonder that at such a time, when he saw Esau coming to kill him and to rob all that he had, he still considered staying in the place of danger by himself, to salvage the little tins. And he did not believe in his life, as it is written, "Then Jacob was very fearful," etc. "And he divided the people... into two camps."

However, this is thoroughly explained with the above-mentioned, because the above-mentioned way—man and beast—was the quality of Jacob the Patriarch, who became an emblem to this quality. It is as it is written in the books: Abraham the Patriarch became an emblem for the quality of love, and Isaac the Patriarch to the quality of fear.

These two qualities are opposites, for one who loves is not afraid and always trusts his loved one, and love covers all transgressions. Conversely, one who fears does not trust, for had he trusted, he would not be afraid at all. But Jacob the Patriarch, the senior from among the Patriarchs, became an emblem of the quality of mercy, meaning these two opposites in the same subject—love and fear together—which is the essence of this quality.

This is the meaning of the verse, "Then Jacob was very fearful," etc. "And he divided the people... into two camps," to leave himself some remains. Also, he sent him gifts, perhaps he would make peace with him.

And you see that his conduct in that regard was the same as a completely ordinary person, for what is the difference if a person is worried of starvation and seeks all kinds of tactics all day long to provide for his livelihood and a bit more, or if he is worried that his enemy might rob him of his possessions and kill him, and does all he can in that regard?

This was Rashi's question: Why was Jacob the Patriarch afraid? After all, He promised him, "And I will keep thee," etc. He explained that he feared lest he would cause the sin. We should be more meticulous and say that he should have said, "lest he caused, and not lest he would cause." This reconciles it, since indeed, Jacob the Patriarch had the complete measure of love, meaning confidence, and he had no doubt at all that the Creator would keep him and that he would lack nothing. Yet he behaved like an ordinary person and pretended to fear, as the animate mind necessitates to find a straightforward tactic for it, that he was very fearful of the 400 men with him. By that, he was seemingly distracted from the confidence, in order to truly fear. Through it, he built his guard the way those who fear an enemy do—he divided the camps and gave presents, etc.

And why did he do it if he were not really afraid, for he trusted in the Creator? It was the fear lest he would cause sin, since in his humbleness, the righteous does not believe in himself, that he will not fall from his degree during the act. For this reason, he prepared every worldly means of salvation against the enemy. And after all that, he assumed in his heart that it was arrogance and treachery, and put his trust in the Creator and prayed to the Creator.

Now we understand why he remained for the little tins, to announce that along with the fear, he had the complete measure of love, completely flawless, and he valued even little tins, for he knew full well that no enemy and foe would touch his possessions, at all.

DIFFERENCE BETWEEN ONE WHO SERVES THE CREATOR AND ONE WHO DOES NOT

This distinguishes between one who serves the Creator and one who does not. One who is truly afraid and does not trust, would not notice the little tins at a time of worry lest an enemy might come and strike mothers with their children, and would destroy everything. But a servant of the Creator, along with the labor and effort due to the fear, knows for certain and trusts His mercy—that all is his and that no stranger will control his possessions. And even at such a time, he is able to watch over the little tins, like the righteous, who are fund of their wealth.

Hence, in the giving of the Torah, we were given the strength, through "remember and keep were said in one utterance. What the mouth cannot say, and the ear to hear and the heart to think and contemplate." This means that it is written that "Remember" is the love and "Keep" is the fear, which are two opposites. They were said to us and given to us as one, to unite them. And although they are really opposite, and it is incomprehensible to the corporeal mind and heart how such a thing can exist in reality, it is the power of the Torah that one who cleaves to it is rewarded with it—being connected and united in his heart, as in the quality of Jacob the Patriarch.

THE *KLIPA* OF ISHMAEL AND THE *KLIPA* OF ESAU

This is what Jacob said during the years of famine: "Why do you fear?" And Rashi interprets, "Why do you fear Ishmael and the children of Esau as though you were satiated?" This is perplexing: The children of Esau dwelled in Seir, and the children of Ishmael in the Paran desert, and what business did they have with them? He had more to worry about the Canaanite and the Hittite, his neighbors in the land.

This is reconciled by the above-mentioned: Rashi made two interpretations: 1—why should you appear satiated, and 2—why should you be slimmed by famine? Now we understand that this is what Jacob had told them: "If you eat to the full, you should fear Ishmael; and if you eat little, you should fear Esau. This means that it is written that Ishmael is the *Sigim* (dross) of silver (love) and Esau is *Sigim* of gold (fear).

And this is what Jacob had taught his sons: if you keep to the quality of love, and trust in the Creator that His hand will not grow short even in the years of famine, you should fear the *Klipa* of Ishmael. And if you hold only to the quality of fear and restrict you eating, you should fear the *Klipa* of Esau, who nurses off of that quality. Hence, best eat to satiation and to unite a thing at that time with the quality of fear: Go down and buy for us from Egypt, for thus you will be saved from both *Klipot*.

Remembering

REMEMBERING AND FORGETTING, KEEPING AND LOSING

During the exile, considered "the female world," the work is in keeping. And one who flaws one's work might lose what he is given. And *Dvekut* (adhesion) in this world is by the force of keeping, and the adornment of the force of keeping is by the elevation of the emotion, as well as the elevation of his wholeness and the strength of his *Dvekut*.

However, in the future, there will be no fear of loss and theft, for death shall be swallowed up forever. And here, the work is limited to "remembering." And although accordingly, one form should have sufficed, the nature of the body is to grow tired of the same form. Hence, forms must be dressed and undressed one at a time, so the body will appear to have a different form every time, to increase the desire. This is similar to blocking the horse's eyes while it is circling the grindstone, so as not to tire it.

This is most profound and grave, since it is simple: His will from the servant is the most praiseworthy. Also, it is known that the closer the work is to nature, the better it is. The rule is that if one of the two lovers' love increases to a complete and utter measure, meaning "natural and complete," the whole force of love will quench in the other.

And although his reason will evidently show the lover's measure of love, his ability to love his friend in return will not grow at all. Moreover, according to the sensation of the totality of the lover, the sense of love will gradually die out in him, for he will not fear him, as his love is absolute. For this reason, the measure of spirituality, the love in the nature of the loved subject, will be annulled and corrupted.

Indeed, His will is to proclaim His love, yet allow room for "expanding the boundaries of love."

These two are opposites, since when his love becomes known, it acquires a mandatory form, like perfect and natural love. Hence, there is zero room for work, to expand the love, since the complete and loyal lover is dissatisfied with the reward of the loved one in return for his love, as it is written, "If you are right, what will you give him?"

Moreover, when the loved one feels that his lover has a desire to love him in return for some reward, that place becomes deficient. This is so because when there is a desire for reward, his love changes when the reward is absent. Thus, the love is not absolute. For this reason, it is not complete and natural, but conditioned, and when the condition is cancelled, the love is cancelled, as in, "a vision of peace, and there is no peace."

It is evidently known that the damned does not cleave to the blessed, as it is written, "Will give wisdom to the wise. And the servitude in adding and expanding the wholeness does not relate at all to one who is deficient, but to the truly complete worker. And to the complete worker, it seems that he has no room for work at all.

This is the meaning of the "remembering," such as when one tells one's loving friend: "Here is a bag full of gems, to show my love." In this way, the loved one strains to accurately count the sum of gems, in order to reveal the love in his own heart, too. In this way, the love itself does not change at all when his work is not counted, since he already has it.

However, to return some reward to the one who loves him, he touches the gems extensively in order to be rewarded with always showing the great measure of the love. In this way, the feelings of love always reach from one to the other and multiply, while the essence is not changed.

This is the meaning of adopting different combinations. Although the essence is the same, not to lose or corrupt even a tiny spark of the potential divulgence of the "hidden forces that always exists in the matter," it appears in new combinations each time, which the corporeal eye has never seen. By that, the matter tastes a new flavor and harnesses itself to suffer and return always and forever. This is similar to many meals, from which the matter is satisfied and wishes to duplicate that form many times, or to couplings, since new flavors are always available for it.

Now you understand the association of matter in a body and soul. Due to the matter, in which "forgetfulness" is rooted, and even worse, by quenching any kind of absolute love, by that it gives the soul room for mandatory work, meaning to return in different combinations every time. Otherwise, the flaw will reach the soul, as well, because of the mask in the roots of matter. And even though the love itself is perfect and complete, it is seemingly covered due to the matter. And by being compelled to return and repeat, the additions increase beyond the fund, and the boundaries of love wondrously expand.

Now you understand the meaning of "the third generation may enter into the assembly of the Lord." In the first generation there was the *Klipa* (shell) of the Egyptian, as though the place was too narrow. This is because although the lover and the loved one are in the desirable wholeness, they lack the room in which to expand and multiply, since due to the suction of matter, the soul must disclose the love in matter, too.

There is no solution for it except to evidently show his love, with great work and great force, since the matter has no other language but emotions. Hence, to the extent of his emotions, his love finds itself compelled to return reward with sublime work and great force. Therefore, when the soul feels His complete and utter love, unconditioned by anything, the work of the matter falls entirely, for "One does not pay for nothing." This is a law in the corporeal nature (for making room, etc.); hence, at that time, the substance strains with its gratitude and subjugation according to its feelings, meaning repeatedly praising and thanking.

And according to the above-mentioned, the matter grows weary of the first combination and the first flavor, and this causes him diminution of sensation, and hence diminution of gratitude, until he stops even this tiny work. And since he remains without work, and sees the absolute love, he places the *Klipa* of the Egyptian from the perspective of the Upper One.

Subsequently, in the second generation, there was the exact same *Klipa* as in the first generation, with the added *Klipa* of the Edomite, meaning not to return or repeat at all, as was the custom in the first generation, which, nonetheless, had a good reason to disclose the feeling from the gratitude.

But "the third generation that are born unto them may enter into the assembly of the Lord," for in the third generation that place is revealed. That is, in the holy *Atik*, the ark-cover was regarded as the mercy seat, and the two were sensed together. This means that making a place for work promptly reveals a great measure of the light of love, that henceforth he will know that prevention of returning a reward prevents the light of love. For this reason, he exerts on until he finds the return of the reward even when he is in a state of wholeness, for he must, against his will, resolve the riddle from the whole, and there is none who is whole. And henceforth, he is a tool ready for work.

We could say that there is room for the complete worker to serve in other bodies to complement them, for this is not completeness in Nature, for Nature mandates revealing, meaning the actual returning of the reward, so he will not be dependent upon the view of others, and lest he will not be found, etc. But one who finds servitude in himself is always serving God, and never rests. And to that extent that light of His love is always endless, never ending.

Two Points

Two points to each aspiration: one in absence, and the other from satiation onward. The difference between them is that the aspiration that stems from fear of absence—while soaring to the highest levels, to the choicest—still, when weary, he settles for the poorest of the poor, and eats to satiation, and to cover *Atik* so it will not be absent. But the aspiration that stems from the point of satiation, meaning that he will not be deficient whatsoever without it, at that time he is not content with little whatsoever, and aspires only to the choicest in reality. And if it is not in that measure, but is rather ordinary, he will not want to work and toil for it at all.

For example: One who is leaning toward playing music is deficient until he acquires it. He will not rest until he has acquired a certain measure of ability to play. And even if he is told that he has no hope of becoming a renowned musician, but only a common one, he will still not give up his aspiration and will settle for less, exerting to at least acquire the little he can acquire. But one who has no inclination toward playing music to begin with, and feels no hunger for this knowledge, should a musician approach him and tell him that he should exert over this lore, he will reply to him even before he has completed his question, "I have no doubt that I will not achieve greatness in this teaching, and to be a common player, is the world deficient without me?"

Indeed, it is embedded by His providence over man that any aspiration that emerges after the point of satiation will not be desirable except for the choicest at that time.

By that you will understand a profound matter, that although the generations are declining in value, they are expanding in desired deficiency and the final correction. It is so because the first generations, who were as people, they themselves had a great and awful deficiency in the prevention of Godly works. For this reason, their aspiration to serve Him emerged from their deficiency. Hence, they did not expand in their aspiration, for fear of losing it entirely, and they were happy and content with the little they attained. This is why they had small and short movements in their work, for because of their recognition of the great value, they settled for little.

This is the meaning of the declining merit of the generations until they arrived at the final shrinkage in our generation, when authors' wisdom is foul and they who fear sin are loathed. In that state the crowd feels content and are not obliged to God's work at all, nor feel any lack in its absence. Even those who do engage in work, it is merely out of habit. They have no thirst or aspiration to finding any speck of knowledge in their work.

And should a sage tell them, "Come, let me teach you wisdom, to understand and to instruct in the word of God," they will promptly reply, "I already know that I will not be as Rashbi and his friends, and let things stay as they are, and I wish I could observe the literal in full." However, it is said about them, "The fathers have eaten sour grapes, and the children's teeth grow blunt," for they engage in Torah and *Mitzvot* (commandments) that are unripe, and their children's teeth will grow utterly blunt, and they wonder why they need this work. It is for you, and not for Him, and you, too, blunt its teeth. This is the form of our generation, with which we are dealing.

But with what is written and explained above, you will understand that in this melting pot we can be very hopeful because henceforth, each learned one whose heart is yearning for the work of God will not be at all among those who are content with less, since the point of his aspiration does not emerge from absence, but from the point of satiation. For this reason, all who come to cling to the Torah and *Mitzvot* will not settle for anything less than being the first in the generation, meaning to actually know his God. He will not want to waste his energy on the work of common folk at all, but only on the choicest—true nearness to God, and to know in his mind that the Creator has chosen him.

Indeed, in our generation we do not find true workers except for those chosen few who have already been endowed with a Godly soul, a part of God above. It is as the poet wrote, "My knee is pure, extending from cistern streams / the name of the one who chooses you, to walk before Him / etc., ...You are before Him as are all who stand before Him / who approach the Lord. My knee, you know the will of the likeminded / the name of knowing your will, and paying each moment."

But they who have not attained this honorable and exalted merit have no love or fear at all in the work. This was not so in previous generations whatsoever, since the servants of the Creator did not aspire for such a high level at all, and each one served the Creator as he understood.

By that you will understand that the correction actually began prior to the reception of the Torah, in the generation of the desert. This is why there was a great awakening in that generation, "It is our wish to see our king," as it is written in the *Midrash* (interpretation). But then they sinned, meaning settled for a messenger, saying, "You will speak to us and we will listen, and let God not speak to us lest we will die."

This is the meaning of the breaking of the tablets and all the exiles. But in the generation of the Messiah, this matter will be corrected because that awakening will return, and when they attain Him, they will no longer sin because they have already suffered doubly for all their sins.

The desired goal is none other than the choicest. This is the meaning of, "And they shall teach no more every man his neighbor, and every man his brother saying, 'Know the Lord,' for they shall all know Me, from the least of them to the greatest of them." This will be the first condition for all who begin the work.

My words do not relate to those who settle for working and laboring to benefit people, and much less so for satisfying their contemptible cravings. Rather, it is for those who feel that it is not worthwhile to toil for people, but only for the Creator.

It is so because there are many factions to judgment day: 1) to satisfy material passions, 2) to benefit people, 3) to improve their own knowledge, or that of others. But all these are forces of concealment of the face, for they are all as nothing compared to the merit of the Creator, of course.

Attaining a True Thing

There is a spiritual substance, on which the letters of the prayer are carved. The substance is the whitest of white parchment. It is also called "white fire," meaning that it is as though that white color comes by fire and turns into fire, crushing and sitting with all its might.

The letters are sparks of fear and love. That is, the deficiency of fear and love are evident and sensed. This is the meaning of the black fire, since that color seems as though it is more deficient and sunken than the rest of the colors. For this reason, in the very beginning, that was the sight.

Initially, the white parchment was seen, which is sufficiently processed with power and with whiteness. This is the meaning of the disclosure of the crown and its glow in *Assiya*. The meaning of *Assiya* is the parchment, as in, "And the foreskin she shall not borrow from her neighbor," in one who "has been joined together." The disclosure of the crown is the true revealed love, up to *Duchra* (male) of *Arich Anpin*, and the shattering is the letters of the fear. Understand that this is truly the book of heaven.

Know that it is true from every angle. For this reason, a man will not truly attain something for which he has no lack, or which is not truly deficient. For this reason, any attainment that comes as a mere extra is not regarded as true attainment, since he is not deficient without it. Hence, there is falsehood in the labor, in the exertion for it as though for something that he truly needs.

This is why external teachings are false wisdom. That is, the work to attain it must be under a complete condition, as though for something that he truly needs and finds. But when he has found and obtained it, he sees that he was not at all deficient without it. Hence, it is a lie and falsehood.

This is not so with the wisdom of serving the Creator. On the contrary, he does not know at all how to sense its absence in its true form. Only when he finds it does he see how deficient he was without it. This is why it is true attainment from every angle.

It is similar to one who pays for an object twice its value. He sighs because his friend had cheated him, and that purchase is false and fraudulent, since the imagination was fooling him.

But regarding the intentions, it is not the doctor who should be asked, but the patient, for he needs sanctity and purity in the work of the Creator, in order to intend, and the intentions will be preparations for his soul for installment of sanctity. Also, we need not ask if the Torah is good, or if morals are good, or if "in all your ways you shall know Him," since the doctor can ask the patient about all that. If he is not in pain then he is certain of his healing, so the patient is the one who knows. This is the meaning of what is written in *The Zohar*: "A man must not look where one shouldn't," meaning that looking does not make him feel sanctity and purity.

ACCEPTING OUR SAGES AS RELIABLE WITNESSES

There are two kinds of servitude—one for the light, and the other for the *Kelim* (vessels)—as it is impossible to speak or to understand degrees in the lights, much less say that one will be rewarded some light, for there is no such thing as part in spirituality, and "a vow that has been slightly broken is broken in its entirety."

(I wonder at the acting mind and the minister of the world together. One gives the power of birth in a seed of adultery in an adulterous, and one bestows stately buildings on false and fictitious foundations.) I am referring to Aristotle, who commanded that he be glorified upon his ascent to heaven for his invention of a false foundation that sufficed as a target for the arrows of his narrow mind, and for the exhaustion of all his spirit. This came to him because he saw in the books of Israel profound wisdom built on the foundations of Kabbalists, and he compared himself to them like a copycat, showing that his merit was as theirs, as he lied about himself. Had the prophecy been true, he would have been prepared for it.

But our way is not his way, and a Kabbalist does not leave a false foundation, as he had left his foundations. Rather, although our sages and their teachings have given us in Kabbalah, but in that, they are as faithful witnesses, eyewitnesses, and nothing more. Instead, they teach us the way by which they were awarded being eyewitnesses. And when we understand, our wisdom will be as theirs, and we will understand a true and real foundation, upon which there is a glorious, eternal building.

The reason for this conduct is that in all things there are a first substance and a first concept. Concerning worldly concepts, which are hidden and immersed in material descriptions, we attain by removing the form, meaning from the first concept to the second concept, and so forth until the desirable concept. For this reason, we come by the first concept very easily, as with the smallest part.

But this is not so with the heavenly. On the contrary, the first concept is the hardest to attain. It is called *Nefesh de Assiya*, and when we acquire the form of *Nefesh de Assiya* through Kabbalah—for attainment is denied of the fool from the heavenly, but through Kabbalah it is possible, through it we learn the heavenly wisdom. At that time we will have the right to attain the received foundation as the nature of the thing that is attained, and it will be possible to reconcile what is received as is natural with all concepts.

But the fictitious foundation of his fictitious wisdom cannot be attained, as "It is enough to come from judgment to be as the judged." Thus, the whole building remains as a false building of eternal disgrace.

THE SOUL OF THE PROSELYTE

The pain that a severed organ feels is during the time of the judgment, the time of the severing. But subsequently, all the pain and deficiency remain in the whole body. Similarly, an organ feels pleasure when it is connected to the new body, but subsequently, the pleasure leaves it as though it has died and returns to the rest of the body. This explains the verse, "And that soul will be cut off from its people," indicating that any pain and deficiency are only for the general public, as though it has been cut off from the people.

Likewise, the pleasure of the soul of the proselyte is only when it connects to the whole nation, the choice of the kind. But when it connects in full, the personal pleasure returns to the whole.

It is an intimation to what people say, "An old man and a child are equal," meaning that one who begins with wisdom, with what is complemented by it, are equal to each other, except for the filling of wisdom, which serves his king and not himself. But the whole question is in the meantime, that it is work of the mind, entirely for oneself and for one's own completion.

For example: The servants of the king and the distinguished ministers of the king all serve the king. This is not so when they learn for their own completion: they work for themselves, like a house full of texts of wisdom and songs of praise. And then when they fall into the hands of the profligates, they only boast with superficial matter that is revealed on paper, and they use it for their contemptible needs ... losing a precious trait from themselves and from the whole world due to the worldliness in them, arousing contempt and wrath.

The heart aches even more when sages see with their own eyes the filthy ones come into the houses of the wisdom of Israel, and take their superficial matter from the words—meaning the beauty of the words—for the work of their hands: vain and sanctimonious allegories.

The orders of the wisdom are established on the foundations of true Kabbalah, attained by the knowledgeable. The form of wisdom is stripped into the work of a craftsman (and in my view were it not for this mirror they would not have had the nerve to fabricate foundations from their hearts), building wittiness on the foundations of falsehood and desolation, as did Aristotle and his company in heaven, and as ... do in corporeality. It is even more so with those who come with disclosed filth, making them targets for his arrows of stupidity, to boast before others as stupid as himself. They cannot be forgiven.

It is an evident example; no deficiency in the world is established in corporeality at all. Rather, every deficiency and wholeness is imprinted in spirituality. That is, in the beginning of wholeness that will be depicted in the world, He will have no need to change any corporeal incident, but only to bless the spiritual. For instance, we see that a man assumes great pains and jolts along the way to gain wealth, even by taking great risks. Then, against your will, the depicting power from the hope of fortune subdues him and turns the evil into great good, until in every bit of his soul he places himself in jeopardy for the sufficient preparation.

Therefore, it is not far at all if the Creator draws near—meaning the reward for the labor, as much as one can. He will not feel any agony or pain in the exertion.

THREE FACTIONS

The Torah is like an entire world, from which three factions enjoy in different ways. The first faction is the masses, who have not been prepared to make any form abstract, unless they have no desire for any form but the first substance from all that fills the world, which come directly to the senses and to the imagination.

The second form is one who has been prepared to be able to make the material form abstract, and to take and enjoy another form, close to spirituality, which is found beneath it. This is an emotional, intellectual delight, meaning from separate concepts imprinted in these material images.

The third form, to the third faction, is one who has been prepared to acquire general forms from separate concepts imprinted in both spiritual and corporeal forms. These tie a thread to a thread, and pull by pull they descend to the deep and rise to the heaven. This form is found after abstracting the above-mentioned second form.

Similarly, three completions come from the Torah to the three above-mentioned factions. The first faction is completed with the first matter. The second faction is completed by form, and the third faction is completed by inclusion, which is abstracting a form from a form, and a thread from a thread. Certainly, one who does not favor people more than matter will certainly not be completed by the Torah more than his will and attainments. This is what Maimonides meant—that one must learn logic before the wisdom of truth.

However, from experience we know and see that there are indirect influence and power in the light in it, which can suddenly lift one above the first faction up to the degree of a man from the third faction. It follows that he works to obtain a needle, and obtains a house full of silver and gold.

This World and the Next World

There is no difference between this world and the next world, except that one is temporary and one is eternal. But there is no possession in this world, or in the next world, that is not a separate spiritual matter. Of course, the measure that one has acquired from this kind in the temporary one will remain his in the eternal one. This is the view of the whole ones, and Maimonides, too, admits it.

However, this cannot be disclosed to the public because they will not listen, and will not pay attention to the work of leaving that small portion to their crass imagination.

It is like a craftsman whose hearing is not influenced by any ordinary sound in the world, except for a great noise. But if all the musicians and singers came together they would provide for his hearing only a crass and noisy sound, and specifically *unpleasant.*

Likewise, it is impossible to speak to the public about anything spiritual except through a chaotic racket. Words of reason will not help them because their souls have not been prepared to enjoy forms that ride atop materialism. Hence, they cling only to the first image of creation that is near them, being the thickness in corporeality. For this reason, words of the next world also necessitate that fine expression be attached to this kind.

Therefore, it is forbidden to speak with them of the intellectual form in the substance of the eternal, for the substance would break, they would not attain that form, and will be denied of both. For this reason, I will make for them a special composition, to provide a general depiction that is close to the truth regarding the form of the Garden of Eden and Hell. Afterward, I will be able to speak of the remaining of the soul with the best among them.

Succinctly speaking, know that the form of this world is a separate, spiritual one, and is not thick or crass, except in relation to the material ones, but not in the form of the Creator. For this reason, he finds all those forms within him.

It follows that at the end of correction, precisely the crass matter will be gone, and the separate forms from these images—both from reality and from the order of existence of reality, such as eating and drinking—will all remain in eternity, since nothing is lost except the matters and their foundations.

But in the forms, there is no loss. They will not suffer at all from the ruin of their first matter, which has already done its part. And if you are one of true form, it is easy to understand how to take off the forms from the filthy materials in the world, such as adultery, gluttony, and self-love, as these forms will remain in spirituality in the form of a separate mind.

They will remain in two discernments: The first discernment is every form toward personal consideration. The second discernment is every form toward a general discernment.

These forms are forever called "carcasses of the wicked," as it is written, "And they shall go forth, and look upon the carcasses of the men who have rebelled against Me." From that we can easily understand the forms of holiness. This is the reward and punishment, and it is felt by the owner in this world, too.

But after the stripping off of the above-mentioned form, there is another abstraction, which is more general. It is called "the world of revival," and "Neither has the eye seen," meaning that even the prophets do not engage in Him, but each one who understands receives from a Kabbalist sage.

By that you will understand the words, "A transgression does not quench a *Mitzvot* (correction, good deed)," since the carrier brings both forms together into the spiritual world. In one he delights, and in the other he is judged. This is the meaning of, "The Creator does not deny the reward from any creation."

And what Maimonides wrote, that there is faith only after the depiction of the operated in one's soul, I wish to say that it is by virtue of the Godly gift, as He discerned regarding the attainment of the light from one another. This does not contradict what I have written.

Here I have explained the completion that comes to the above-mentioned first and second factions. But as for what comes to the third faction, I have implied but did not explain.

The Meaning of the Chaf in Anochi[3]

Malchut that is clothed in the worlds is called *Ani* (me/I). It hangs down to *Assiya*, which is the separation, where each person feels as a separate entity, sensing the "self," and by its expansion wishes to conquer the entire world for one's own will and pleasure. This is the power of the shattering in *Assiya*, "I will rule," meaning from holy sparks that were not yet sorted. It is called "the serpent's skin," which is the good and bad in the *Noga* shell.

There are two souls in the creature, in which one acquires. They clothe in two spirits: the "vital soul" and the "intellectual soul." One is from the *Noga* shell, and one is a part of God above. It is also called, "The soul of every flesh is its blood," and this is the vital soul. The intellectual soul is the point in the heart (prior its completion, as in, "And my heart is awake"). And because the vital soul extends from the *Noga* shell, it is called "coincidental," the opposite of eternal. The holy soul is called "eternal," which is a part of God above.

---

3   *Chaf* is a letter in the word *Anochi* (me).

The Difference between the Bodies of Idol Worshippers and the Bodies of Israel

Now we should scrutinize according to what is written, "One does not lift a finger below unless one is mentioned above." It is also written that "the nations are as a drop of a bucket, and are counted as the small dust of the balance." How can both be observed, for it is obvious that Providence and the dust of the balance or the drop of a bucket do not go together, as there is no thought without an action in the Creator, or an action without a purpose even in people?

Indeed, this is why there is a difference between the bodies of idol worshippers and the bodies of Israel. The body of a servant of the Creator is judged by Him in private Providence, to the Creator's will, the desired purpose. For this reason, although the body is an inconsequential hell from its onset, it still appeared in the Creator's thought as a tool for work. But the bodies of idol worshippers, which are unfit for serving the Creator, and which are not eternal, private Providence is unified in them only in general, and not in particular. It is as one who weighs meat on scales: he knows in his mind that over time some dust will be left on the balance, but that thought is not regarded as such because it is without an intention, for why would he need the dust, and he does not need the body at all!

Let me offer an example: A person buys a box with letters for printing, and gives them to the worker to print books with them. It follows that all the printing is done by the landlord's supervision, although he is not the operator.

But it is one thing with motionless letters, for which they are not under the landlord's monitoring, as they are never his intention, and all the thoughts regarding the above kind were only on actions, but not on emptiness and nothingness. And also, the merit of the landlord is not diminished by inactive letters, since he is not the operator, naturally. However, the merit of the operator does indeed diminish because he is idle and makes little use of the blessing that extends from the direct preparation that he gives to him.

The lesson is that the printing operator is the vital soul, which extends from the *Noga* shell with two forms—good or bad—and the points are taken from the point in the heart, while the body of the letters are from the spaces of the whole world.

ANI (ME/I)—ANOCHI (ALSO ME/I)

If the printer draws near to good neighbors, who give him ways and hints of good combinations, that printer acquires a new form, called "one golden pan of ten shekels, full of incense." The form of the initial feeling of the *Ani* is swallowed in a new form of *Anochi*, and this is the reward for his good act. At that time his merit reaches the merit of the author, like an uneducated printer who prints books. Over time, by looking in the books for his own needs, becomes educated and writes books like his prior landlords, as well as gives his books to other printers, and raises their pay.

But if the printer is in a bad environment, and he is made to print bad combinations, punctuated from the shell of the point in their hearts, the left hollow, he becomes as lost and forsaken as they are, like the dust of a bucket.

A COINCIDENTAL FORM AND AN ETERNAL FORM

By that you can understand that the printer and the box of letters are all coincidental and not eternal, and the author does not take them into consideration in and of themselves at all. It is just as one who hires an employee to do some work does not regard the beauty of his face or his appearance, for they are not the issue. What is important is his strength and loyalty, and on that the landlord's guidance focuses, and not on the rest of his qualities, which are merely coincidental in regard to him (although they are to be noticed for other discernments: for mating, and for being liked by friends, and this is regarded as the general). The focus of his author's thought is in direct, undistorted combinations due to work, so they are fit to disclose the wisdom concealed in those combinations, so all who sees them will acquire his form by himself and will become as wise as he. His intention to create a new creation, as spiritual as Himself, is similar to the desire of corporeal beings—man, fowl, and beast—to preserve the species.

This is the meaning of the keeping of the soul for eternity, regarded as the one *Chaf* (one of the Hebrew letters) that the printer purchased. It is the "new *Anochi*," for then it acquires a new form, as the author himself, and makes by himself good and steadfast combinations, full of blessing and light. The combinations remain for eternity as vessels of *Hochma*, and his one *Chaf*, which is his *Anochi*, is filled abundantly with pleasures of joy, gladness, and preciousness, which are his lot for eternity.

It follows that knowing and choosing come as one, since the printer has no freedom of choice, for he is printing other people's books and not his own. However, when he is rewarded with taking off that form and putting on the form of *Anochi*, he becomes one of the chosen among the nation, chosen by the God above, as it is written in the Midrash, "'And therefore choose life,' as one who takes his son's hands, places them on a good portion, and tells him, 'Choose this for yourself,' as it is written, 'And therefore choose life.'"

We might say that his knowledge necessitates the act, and if he knew that the *Ani* would acquire the *Anochi*, then he would be compelled to acquire it. If so, what is the reward for his actions? This is the meaning of "If you walk contrary to Me, I will walk with rage against you," to teach you that the acquired form is a new spiritual being that is made by taking off the corporeal form. Any printer who gives his coincidental form and is ready for the Creator, the Creator is ready to take off his coincidental form and replace it with a new, spiritual one, creating in him a new heart and a new spirit.

This is so with one who prints good books, and focuses on benefiting from them in eternity. But with one who prints bad combinations, who focuses on enjoying them and what has already been imprinted in him at birth, he clings to the pollution (lit. nocturnal ejaculation) in an inconsequential, passing world. And therefore, "I, too, will walk against you with rage."

Thus, it is clear to you that this question has nothing to do with spirituality, for it is impossible to derive from corporeality. For example, if the Creator knows that Reuben will have a son, then Reuben must have a son even without the coupling of male and female. Such a thing is unthinkable, since we should say according to the nonsense of this question that He knew everything you'd do after all the scrutinies, and that you are compelled.

And the printer who clings to the pollution necessarily falls under the rage, as well, and we should not say that he does not deserve to be punished, since he has no choice or free will, for the punishment is the form he is in, as in prior to creation and absence. It is not a punishment from the Creator, but that He did not create one who does not want to be created and take off his coincidental form and adopt a new, spiritual, eternal form.

In that regard, we could ask about the affliction of the souls in Hell. This relates to the point in the heart before it is included in its root. It must emit its pollution from the material world, which is a bitter punishment for it, and not revenge. On the contrary, it is a great salvation. This is very deep and understand it as Arvut [(mutual guarantee) could also mean "pleasantness"], as general.

NO PLURALITY IN THE ESSENCE OF ETERNITY

...Indeed, one who sows for bread is not meticulous in choosing the place, the particular place, but in the positive relation between the place and his seed, and any place where he sows and finds sufficient bread, and he is content without profit and without even a little of the value of the place itself, for it is the same everywhere. This is the meaning of what one must say, "The world was created for me," since the whole world is rewarding for him. The whole world was created only to command this, since there is no plurality in the essence of eternity, and all the forms of the souls are one and unique essence. It is so because there is no "part" in spirituality, and the whole issue of deficiency and correction is a new creation made by taking off the old form. These are the entertainments of the Creator, as in, "The king is glorified in the multitude of the people."

Understand that there is no plurality of entertainment in the Creator in the general redemption of the entire world at once, more than the redemption of one soul at one time. It is so because remote people and bodies were not added without time, for one at a time is called "two couplings," of heaven and of earth. Two people at one time are called "one coupling," and the soul is jointly theirs, completely equally, without subtraction or addition, as in luck, time, cause, or age, for all who are born at the same time share the same sign (fortune).

Thus, it is clear that the main purpose of the creation of the 6,000 years is to multiply generations and times in which the couplings will change and multiply, but not to multiply bodies. Otherwise, it will be difficult, for He could have created all the bodies of the 6,000 years in one year. Moreover, it is known ... so the bodies are renewed, and the first ones themselves incarnate and come in time and in generations, meaning their "vital soul," which is the root of the speaking.

Therefore, he does not care at all which body will disclose the desire as long as the desire is disclosed, by whomever it is disclosed. It is just as it does not matter what the face of the printer looks like, as long as the book is printed. But the printers themselves, who are numerous in the world, are as the drop of a bucket and the dust of the scales, consumed and lost by their own rage. However, we do need a printer who is capable in his work, and anyone who takes on the work takes his reward from the complete one, and knowing does not necessitate his face in particular, but rather everyone whose heart is kind will raise a donation to the Lord, and the more one hurries, the better it is, in and of itself.

CREATION IS PRIMARILY THE ETERNITY IN CREATION

Explanation: The Creator is omnipotent, and therefore although the creatures are as beasts, still, one who is rewarded with annulling one's will before the Creator's will, He gives him and creates within him a new spirit and a new heart, and enthrones him over all His works, as in, "By Me kings reign." It is similar to a viceroy, to whom all the governance of the state is given, and one who is favored by that rewarded one, He takes him from the providence attributed to the shells, and places him under the Providence that is established for eternity, and He will do the will of those who fear Him. This is the meaning of, "As I create worlds, so the righteous create worlds."

It is so because creation is primarily about the eternity in creation, where the eternal in the first creation of this world, meaning *Adam HaRishon*, the Creator's creation, is attributed to the Creator. But from Adam onward that creation is given to the righteous in each generation. They are the ones leading the worlds as they wish and desire, and "a righteous sentences and the Creator executes."

Know that for this reason the providence of corporeality need not change at all, since spirituality is not bounded by the corporeal boundary, and it is fitting for completion over all the boundaries in the corporeal reality.

This is why the world is filled with immeasurable corpses, to such an extent that even if 600,000 righteous are established, they will still be able to engage in creating new worlds. However, everything follows the internality, which is Providence, where the righteous establishes and the Creator executes. And the sense of surplus on that will be as the drop of a bucket or as the dust of the scales, and Nature cannot regard what is worthless.

The vital soul is regarded as corrupted and about to be burned, without the value of being. It is called "pollution" (lit. nocturnal ejaculation) to imply that the sensation of being of his own self is under rage of pollution, and incidental. However, a soul that acquires a part of God above is called "being," and this is the meaning of "to give to those who love Me being (substance), and to fill their treasuries." Only of this being can we speak, and not of all the shells that preceded its making, whose being is merely coincidental, present during the work, and finally destroyed. The heaven and earth will wear out like a garment, and only the acquired desire will remain for all eternity.

By that "being" is the plurality according to the generations and times, as incarnations. For this reason there is no division in the innovation of the "being" between one body and all the bodies in the world, since analysis and plurality are dependent on "times."

The Wisdom of Israel Compared to External Wisdoms

THE STANDARD BY WHICH TO EVALUATE A WISDOM

The value of any wisdom in the world is according to the purpose that it yields. This is the goal to which all the scrutinies aim. Therefore, a wisdom without some purpose is inconceivable except for infants playing games, since to pass the time they come and this is their purpose, according to their value. For this reason, a wisdom is not evaluated by keenness and proficiency, but according to the merit of the purpose that it yields.

You therefore find that any external wisdom is only for the purpose of corporeality, which is sure to be gone today or tomorrow. In that case, it is sufficient for the subject to be as the predicate.

And although the wisdom has many advantages over these subjects, for wherever it is, it is nonetheless a spiritual element, but we have already said that it is evaluated by the purpose, which is its persistence for eternity. And if the purpose is transitory and fleeting, it is lost along with it.

Now we have a standard by which to gauge the significance of the wisdom of Israel compared to an external wisdom. It concerns only the understanding of the ways of the Creator over His creations and adhering to Him. It follows that the very essence of this wisdom relies on the Creator. And because the importance of the Creator compared to His creations, which He has created, is inconceivable, the merit of the wisdom of Israel compared to external wisdoms is also inconceivable.

And because the very essence of our wisdom is ever valid and eternal, our entire wisdom will also remain eternal. And because it concerns favoring approaching the Creator, which is the finest goal that can ever be perceived, one who engages in it, and certainly one who is rewarded with it, is the finest of the finest among the speaking species.

FOOLS HAVE NO DESIRE

But fools have no desire. Therefore, the house of Israel are few, as our sages have written, "A thousand people commence with the Bible [Torah], a hundred with the Mishnah, ten with the Talmud, and one of them comes out (to teach)."

"I saw the children of the ascent, and they are few." There are many reasons for it. But the main one is that all who begin with it wish to taste it in full, and the smallest of the measures of those fools is to at least know the righteousness of His guidance.

There is a sort of a must to know, and it can be made known, according to the spirit of the fool. But "What shall we do to our sister in the day when she is spoken for"? After all, our wisdom can be interpreted in every way, except for the way of the stomach, for the subjects of this wisdom do not need the way of the stomach. This is what we wanted to clarify, and we shall clarify it in a separate essay, for it is the beginning of the confusion and its end.

YOU SHALL LIVE A SORROWFUL LIFE

Go and see, and you will find that there is one prerequisite to every wisdom, even to external wisdoms: "Live a sorrowful life." It is a well-known thing that anyone who has merited the title "sage" disparages every worldly pleasure. According to the measure of the abstention that one's soul chooses to tolerate due to the affliction of pursuing the wisdom, to that very extent does one find it.

Thus, we should ask one question regarding all the sages in the world together: Every love emerges from one's own flesh and self, and returns to one's own self and flesh. Thus, how do all the sages fail in loving wisdom, whose beginning and end is nothing but the labor of the flesh?

Indeed, any experienced person knows that the greatest of all the world's imaginable pleasures is to win people's favor. Obtaining this coveted thing is worth making every effort and worldly concession. This is the magnet to which the finest in every generation are drawn, and for which they trivialize the whole of the worldly life.

Also, each wisdom comes with its own terminology, whose progenitors have established and by which they explained their wishes. That language is a mediator—close to the wisdom itself and close to the ones engaging in it—since there is a great advantage to it in that it uses few words to explain many things.

THE CARRIERS OF THE WISDOM OF TRUTH, AND THE CARRIERS OF AN EXTERNAL WISDOM

According to the merit of the wisdom of truth, it is evident that the prerequisite that applies to any wisdom applies to it, as well, namely to disparage worldly life. But in addition to that is the need to disparage the collective magnet—people's favor.

An external sage disparages worldly life in order to be saved from wasting one's precious time on obtaining it. Such is the case with all the fools—due to their fondness of worldly life, they waste their time on it. The sage is saved from them like a fugitive due to his choice to ridicule worldly life. In return for this he will obtain wisdom during that same time.

By that you can deduce regarding the sages of truth, that as long as they do not disparage the collective magnet—winning people's favor—they are not at all ready to attain this wisdom. That person will waste the time on winning people's favor and will as the fools who waste their time on worldly life. Such a person's heart is not free to attain a pure and clean wisdom, and is unfit to win the Creator's favor, and this is simple.

Now you can understand why our wisdom was undesirable to people in the world, and why they do not regard it even as an inferior wisdom. They are mistaken because of the different subjects, for the whole purpose of external wisdom is to win people's favor. Therefore, they exert to cloak their wisdom with a superficial garment that even the fools will accept, since they are the majority, and they are the ones who make every famous person famous.

CONCEALING THE WISDOM OF TRUTH FROM THE FOOLS

But the sages of truth had no interest in showing part of the wisdom to an extent that the fools will accept, since these fools have no desire. I wish to say that even if the sages of the generation strove to educate them about the truth so they would accept it, still, not because of that will they commence with the Torah.

The fool has no desire unless by the revealing of his heart and matters that are close to him, namely that relate to worldly pleasures. I have already explained that the fool does not remain in folly due to his loathing of the wisdom, but due to his nearness to people's delights, for his whole life will not suffice to satisfy half his wishes. For this reason, he has no time for wisdom, even if he likes it, and even if the sages who are famous in external wisdoms were regarded as fools and worldly compared to this wisdom due to their nearness to winning people's favor, which in relation to this wisdom is tantamount to worldly lusts and bodily satiations.

OUR SAGES DID NOT DISCLOSE DEVELOPMENT FROM THE WISDOM OF TRUTH

Because of it, our sages did not disclose to the fools any development from the wisdom of truth, for it is a great offense, as our sages said, "As one is commanded to say what is heard, one is also commanded not to say what is not heard." And it is also written in *The Zohar* in many places: "Woe if I say; woe if I do not say. If I say, the unworthy will know how to serve their master," etc. Because of the importance of the wisdom—to avoid needlessly making it empty words in the mouths of the fools, as those who are fed by the passion of their hearts will not be nourished by the brightness of the *Shechina* [Divinity] for certain, as our sages said, "All whose heart is proud," etc.

This is the reason why each time the wicked *Malchut* spreads over the generation our holy Torah is promptly sentenced to be burned, as has happened to us several times, and even in our generation. It was so because they had loathed the wisdom of His uniqueness, which is always sour in the eyes of the fools, as I have explained that they do not find any purpose in it by which to satisfy their foul lusts. On the contrary, they are robbed because of it, for they cannot enjoy, and they do not enjoy the incest in public—the only thing that pacifies their hearts.

Four Worlds

Four Forms: Point, Line, Area, Cube / The Act of *Mitzvot* /
Three Covenants / *Otiot* and *Nekudot* (Letters and Points) /
Atzmut (Self/Essence) and *Kelim* (Vessels)

A ttainment, as a whole, comes by **matter and form**, whose
beginning is **the being**. Also, the attained sustains the "being,"
which is devoid of matter and form. This is considered "the
four worlds," perceived in everything that exists (meaning, a world
is giving and receiving), and all our engagements are in matter and
form, in creating and doing, on which the work relies.

This is so because creation is their whole, and it does not quite
expand in the perception of the mind. Also, the form essentially
divides the doing, meaning the materials, into many details, each
with its own unique form. And the mind thoroughly cleaves to it
and abundantly expands through it, to distinguish one thing from
another, to divide and to tell this from that. This is the purpose of
the work: to know the advantage of Light over darkness in every
detail that exists, as it is written, "All is determined by thought."

FOUR FORMS: POINT, LINE, AREA, CUBE

All the forms in the world are **points, lines, areas**, and **cubes**,
which is an area multiplied from all directions. These four forms
contain all the types of shapes in the world, and all that exists

on land exists in the ocean of wisdom, meaning in the Upper Worlds, to which this world is but an imprint, cascading from the spiritual worlds Above, which we are destined to attain in the next world.

However, during the work, in our existence in this world, we have no other attainments, unless they are clothed in corporeal dresses, which are corporeal shapes without which we are unable to perceive and understand anything.

Hence, we attain all the *Vavs* in the name *HaVaYaH*, which contain all the shapes in the world, which are **point, line—Yod, Vav**, and in the two **Heys—area and cube**. The last **Hey** is the disclosure of the first **Hey**, but **Heys** are more—**area and cube**, where the last **Hey** is the disclosure of the first **Hey** but more materialized, meaning a form that occupies space. This is not so with the three other forms, which do not take up any space.

This is the meaning of... meaning one part of the created beings in this world is in the dark without a **name** for people to examine, as this is what stems from Him, since it seems to be against His will. But in general, we know that His kingdom rules over all, and when the worker comes to that thing and examines it, this, too, is given from His abundance. Thus, it sanctifies His Name and raises the holy spark from the *Klipa*, which is the whisperer that separates the Champion.

And to the extent of the scrutiny and the awareness in the thought of the worker, the "Name" grows and sanctifies.

In general, all of Israel believe and unite with His Name twice, every day with love. But that unity should appear in the thought of the worker with every... and in complete recognition. This is called raising *Mayin Nukvin* and the descent of *Mayin Duchrin*, since the labor... which is the *MAD*, repeatedly rises, adding to one's awareness every time until... And this worker becomes a partner to the Creator in the act of creation. And as the Creator creates worlds, he, too, creates worlds.

This is considered a full world—giving and receiving, which is called a world, that is, heaven and earth. This is the meaning of the phrase that the righteous always create new heaven and earth.

THE ACT OF MITZVOT

Although in truth, all is determined by thought, actual deeds from below must be evoked, as well. This is because everything must expand through the actual world of *Assiya* (action), which is the actual disclosure, when holiness and the revelation of His kingdom spread through *Assiya*, and "everyone will recognize," etc. Hence, the complete correction is to actually evoke the uniqueness of the Creator in everything, and this is the essence of the whole act of *Mitzvot*.

THREE COVENANTS

Now you understand the three covenants: covenant of the eyes, covenant of the tongue, and circumcision. This means that unification and raising *Mayin Nukvin* are done primarily in one's thought. Still, this recognition is not completed there before one's internal recognition appears outwardly. The Master's Face is desired and appears in three places: a) covenant of the eyes, b) covenant of the tongue, and c) circumcision, each according to its own discernment. Some things are completed in what cleaves to it by what one sees, and some things are completed by words or real actions.

With circumcision, less is better. And the evidence is that the work with the eyes is good, whether before oneself or before a friend. But it must not be so with circumcision; it is a great offence. About his wife, too, it was said, "as though unwillingly." The reason is that man is the last degree of all the holiness; hence, the *Klipa* clothes his NHY. This is the meaning of warming, becoming fire, fire for the Name (the letters *Yod, Hey*) has risen.

Perhaps this is the meaning of "A handsome maiden with no eyes." This is because it is known that each *Partzuf* clothes the NHY of the Upper *Partzuf* and is considered the *Peh* (mouth) of the lower one, the *Yesod* (foundation) of the Upper One. Hence, we could say that the *Eynaim* (eyes) of the lower one are at the place of *Yesod* of the Upper One. It turns out that the *Eynaim* of the Upper One are completely missing.

It follows that we clothe the *Kedusha* (holiness) only in the form of **our eye and mouth**. Hence, all our unifications are only in those two covenants: **mouth** and **eye**. Know, that the Creator has instilled force in those two covenants—to give all the shapes of the world from one to the other—meaning teacher and student, in text or orally. It turns out that there is power in the study to receive all the teachings in the world through text, as well as in the mouth—to give all the abundance in the world to one's friend.

...The creation of the worlds was only for the Torah and for... seemingly a sublime and abstruse wisdom, to bring it to Israel. For this reason, he used... the above-mentioned three covenants. This is the meaning of the written Torah and the oral Torah, where the writing... affects, etc., and all is one.

OTIOT AND NEKUDOT (LETTERS AND POINTS)

Transfer their influence is through *Otiot* (letters) and *Nekudot* (points). The eye perceives only letters and points, from which the heart understands. Similarly, the mouth is affected only by letters. This is why it is called "***Lev***" (heart, as well as 32 in

Gematria), since it receives the *Hochma* (wisdom) through the thirty-two paths of bestowal—twenty-two letters and ten points—as this is essentially the shapes of the world and what is in it with respect to the boundaries of the wisdom and the sustenance of the world.

This is the meaning of the four-letter-name *HaVaYaH*, which contains every shape in speech and in text, since the construction of the letters is from points and lines: each point is a *Tzimtzum* (restriction) and each lines an expansion.

ATZMUT (SELF/ESSENCE) AND KELIM (VESSELS)

Atzmut (Self/Essence) revolves around two kinds of Lights: 1) relating to the Operator, and 2) relating to the operated. This is the meaning of male and female, line and *Reshimo*, soul and body, king and kingship, Creator and Divinity, mercy and judgment—the work is completed with the true union.

The *Atzmut* governs and appears on the *Kli* to the extent of the awakening of the *Kli* and its preparation. This is the meaning of the states of ZON, since the whole issue of *Nukva* is only about those who receive according to their preparation in their work.

These two discernments are distinguished in all the creatures. And the nature of the *Atzmut* is that it appears to the eye only by the *Kli* in which it is clothed. It is recognized through the *Kli*, and almost no part of the *Atzmut* is perceived, but only the *Kli* that clothes the *Atzmut*, "and from my flesh."

And since the closeness of the Creator to His creatures is recognized by the Torah, as in the **gift**, "from Mattanah to Nahaliel,"[4] which is discerned as the actual Creator. One can say that one knows Him even though there is neither perception

---

4   Translator's note: In Hebrew, *Mattanah* means "gift" and *Nahaliel* means "rivers of God."

nor thought in Him at all, for if you say that you know your twin, you do not know more than his *Kli*, for his *Atzmut* is clothed within him.

And of course, all the words of Torah and prayer in which His guidance is evident are said to be the actual revelation of Godliness and natural recognition. This is the meaning of "The Torah, the Creator, and Israel are one."

The Teaching of the Kabbalah and Its Essence

What is the wisdom of Kabbalah? As a whole, the wisdom of Kabbalah concerns the revelation of Godliness, arranged on its path in all its aspects—those that have emerged in the worlds and those that are destined to be revealed, and in all the manners that can ever appear in the worlds, to the end of time.

THE PURPOSE OF CREATION

Since there is no act without some purpose, it is certain that the Creator had a purpose in the Creation set before us. And the most important thing in this whole diverse reality is the sensation given to the animals—that each of them feels its own existence. And the most important sensation is the noetic sensation, given to man alone, by which one also feels what is in one's other—the pains and comforts. Hence, it is certain that if the Creator has a purpose in this Creation, its subject is man. It is said about him, "All of the Lord's works are for him."

But we must still understand what was the purpose for which the Creator created this lot? Indeed, it is to elevate him

155

to a Higher and more important degree, to feel his God like the human sensation, which is already given to him. And as one knows and feels one's friend's wishes, so will he learn the words of the Creator, as it is written about Moses, "And the Lord spoke unto Moses face to face, as a man speaketh unto his friend."

Any person can be as Moses. Undoubtedly, anyone who examines the evolution of Creation before us will see and understand the great pleasure of the Operator, whose operation evolves until it acquires that wondrous sensation of being able to converse and deal with one's God as one speaks to one's friend.

From Above Downwards

It is known that the end of the act is in the preliminary thought. Before one begins to think about how to build a house, one contemplates the apartment in the house, which is the purpose. Subsequently, one examines the blueprint to make it suitable for this task.

So it is with our matter. Once we have learned about the purpose, it is also clear to us that all the conducts of Creation, in its every corner, inlet, and outlet, are completely prearranged for the purpose of nurturing the human species from its midst, to improve its qualities until it can sense Godliness as one feels one's friend.

These ascensions are like rungs of a ladder, arranged degree-by-degree until it is completed and achieves its purpose. And you should know that the quality and quantity of these rungs is set in two realities: 1) the existence of material substances, and 2) the existence of spiritual concepts.

In the language of Kabbalah, they are called "**from Above downwards**" and "**from below Upwards.**" This means that the corporeal substances are a sequence of disclosure of His Light **from Above downwards**—from the first source, when a measure of Light was cut off from His Essence, and was restricted *Tzimtzum* by *Tzimtzum* (restriction by restriction) until the corporeal world was formed off it, with corporeal creatures at its very bottom.

FROM BELOW UPWARDS

Afterwards begins an order of **from below Upwards**. These are all the rungs of the ladder by which the human race develops and climbs up to the purpose of creation. These two realities are explained in their every detail in the wisdom of Kabbalah.

NECESSITY TO STUDY KABBALAH

An opposer might say, "Therefore, this wisdom is for those who have already been rewarded with a measure of Godly revelation, but what necessity can the majority of the people have for knowing this sublime wisdom?"

Indeed, there is a common opinion that the prime goal of religion and the Torah is only the cleansing of actions, that all that is desired concerns observing the physical *Mitzvot* (commandments), without any additions or anything that should result from it. Had that been so, those who say that studying the revealed and practical actions alone is sufficient would be right.

Yet, this is not the case. Our sages have already said, "Why should the Creator mind if one slaughters at the throat or at the back of the neck? After all, the *Mitzvot* were only given to cleanse people." Thus, there is a purpose beyond the observance of the actions, and the actions are merely preparations for this purpose. Hence, clearly, if the actions are not arranged for the desired goal, it is as if nothing exists. And it is also written in *The Zohar*: "A *Mitzva* (commandment) without an aim is like a body without a soul." Hence, the aim, too, should accompany the act.

Also, it is clear that the aim should be a true aim worthy of the act, as our sages said about the verse, "'And I will set you apart from the peoples, that ye should be Mine,' so your separation will be for My Name. Let not one say, 'Pork is impossible.' Rather, let one say 'it is possible, but what can I do, my Father in Heaven has sentenced me.'"

Thus, if one avoids pork because of abomination or because of some bodily harm, this aim does not help at all for it to be considered a *Mitzva*, unless one has the unique and proper intention that the Torah forbade. So it is with every *Mitzva*, and only then is one's body gradually purified by observing the *Mitzvot*, which is the desired purpose.

Hence, the study of **physical conducts** is not enough; we need to study those things that produce **the desirable intention**, to observe everything with faith in the Torah and in the Giver of the Torah, that there is a Judgment and there is a Judge.

Who is so foolish as not to understand that faith in the Torah and in reward and punishment, which have the power to yield this great thing, require much study in the proper books? Thus, even before the act, a study that purifies the body is required, to grow accustomed to faith in the Creator, His Law, and His Providence. Our sages said about that, "I have created the evil inclination; I have created for it the Torah as a spice." They did not say, "I have created for it the *Mitzvot* as a spice," since "your guarantor needs a bondsman himself," as the evil inclination desires licentiousness and will not let him keep the *Mitzvot*.

Torah as a Spice

The Torah is the only spice to annul and subdue the evil inclination, as our sages said, "The Light in it reformed them."

THE MAJORITY OF THE WORDS OF THE TORAH ARE FOR STUDY

This reconciles why the Torah speaks at length on parts that do not concern the practical part but only the study, meaning the introduction to the act of Creation. These are the whole of the book of *Beresheet* (*Genesis*), *Shemot* (*Exodus*), most of *Devarim* (*Deuteronomy*), and, needless to say, legends and commentaries. Yet, since they are what the Light is stored in, his body will be purified, the evil inclination subdued, and he will come to faith in the Torah and in reward and punishment. This is the first degree in the observance of the work.

COMMANDMENT IS A CANDLE, AND TEACHING IS LIGHT

It is written, "For the commandment is a candle, and the teaching is light." As one who has candles but no light to light them sits in the dark, one who has *Mitzvot* but no Torah sits in the dark. This is because the Torah is Light, by which the darkness in the body is illuminated and lit up.

NOT ALL PORTIONS OF THE TORAH ARE OF EQUAL LIGHT

According to the above-mentioned power in the Torah, that is, considering the measure of **Light** in it, it is certain that the Torah should be divided into degrees, according to the measure of **Light that one can receive** from studying it. Clearly, when one ponders and contemplates words of Torah that pertain to the revelation of the Creator to our fathers, they bring the examiner more **Light** than when examining practical matters.

159

Although they are more important with respect to the actions, with respect to the Light, the revelation of the Creator to our fathers is certainly more important. Anyone with an honest heart who has tried to ask to receive the **Light** of the Torah will admit to that.

NECESSITY AND UNFOLDING OF THE EXPANSION OF THE WISDOM

Since the whole of the wisdom of Kabbalah speaks of the revelation of the Creator, naturally, there is none more successful teaching for its task. This is what the Kabbalists aimed for—to arrange it so it is suitable for studying.

And so they studied in it until the time of concealment (it was agreed to conceal it for a certain reason). However, this was only for a certain time, and not forever, as it is written in *The Zohar*, "This wisdom is destined to be revealed at the end of days, and even to children."

It follows that the above-mentioned wisdom is not at all limited to the language of Kabbalah, as its essence is a spiritual Light that emerges from His Essence, as it is written, "Can thou send forth lightnings, that they may go, and say unto thee: 'Here we are,'" referring to the two above ways: **from Above downwards and from below Upwards.**

These matters and degrees expand according to a language suitable for them, and they are truly all the beings in this world and their conducts in this world, which are their branches. This is so because "You have not a blade of grass below that does not have an angel above, which strikes it and tells it, 'Grow!'" Thus, the worlds emerge from one another and are imprinted from one another like a seal and imprint. And all that is in one is in the other, down to the corporeal world, which is their last branch, but contains the world Above it like an imprint of a seal.

Thus, it is easy to know that we can speak of the Higher Worlds only by their corporeal, lower branches, which extend from them, or of their conducts, which is the language of the Bible, or by secular teachings or by people, which is the language of Kabbalists, or according to agreed upon names. This was the conduct in the Kabbalah of the *Geonim* since the concealment of *The Zohar*.

Thus, it has been made clear that the revelation of the Creator is not a one-time disclosure, but an ongoing matter that is revealed over a period of time, sufficient for the disclosure of all the great degrees that appear from Above downwards and from below Upwards. On top of them, and at the end of them, appears the Creator.

It is like a person proficient in all the countries and people in the world, who cannot say that the whole world has been revealed to him before he has completed his examination of the last person and the last country. Until one has achieved that, one has not attained the whole world.

Similarly, the attainment of the Creator unfolds in preordained ways. The seeker must attain all those ways in both the Upper and the lower. Clearly, the Upper Worlds are the important ones here, but they are attained together because there is no difference in their shapes, only in their substance. The substance of a Higher World is purer, but the shapes are imprinted from one another, and what exists in the Higher World necessarily exists in all the worlds below it, since the lower one is imprinted by it. Know that these realities and their conducts, which the seeker of the Creator attains, are called "degrees," since their attainment is arranged one atop the other, like rungs of a ladder.

SPIRITUAL EXPRESSIONS

The spiritual has no image, hence it has no letters to contemplate with. Even if we declare in general that it is Simple Light, which descends and extends to the seeker until one clothes and attains it in the amount sufficient for His revelation, this, too, is a borrowed expression. This is so because everything that is called "Light" in the spiritual world is not like the light of the sun or candlelight.

What we refer to as Light in the spiritual world is borrowed from the human mind, whose nature is such that when a doubt is resolved in a person, one discovers a kind of abundance of light and pleasure throughout the body. This is why we sometimes say "the light of the mind," although this is not so. The light that shines in those parts of the substance of the body that are unsuitable for receiving resolved scrutinies is certainly something inferior to the mind. Hence, those lower, inferior organs can receive it and attain it, too.

Yet, to be able to name the mind by some name, we call it "the light of the mind." Similarly, we call the elements of the reality of the Upper Worlds "Lights," as they bring those who attain them abundance of light and pleasure throughout the body, from head to toe. For this reason, we may call one who attains "clothing," for he has clothed that Light.

We might ask, "Would it not be more correct to call them by names used in scrutiny, such as observation and attainment, or to express oneself with expressions that emphasize the phenomena of the noetic mind?" The thing is that it is nothing like the conducts of the noetic phenomena, since the mind is a particular branch among all the elements of reality. Hence, it has its own ways of manifestation.

This is not so with degrees, as they are a complete whole, which contains all the elements that exist in a world. Each element has its own particular ways. For the most part, the perception of matters in degrees is similar to the perception of animate bodies: when one attains some essence, one attains the whole of it, from head to toe.

If we judge by the laws of the noetic mind, we can say that he has attained everything he could attain in that essence, and even if he contemplated it for another thousand years, he would not add to it even an iota. Yet, in the beginning it is very similar to... meaning he sees everything but understands none of what he sees. Yet, by the passing of time he will have to attain additional matters, similar to *Ibur* (conception), *Yenika* (nursing), *Mochin* (adulthood), and a second *Ibur*. At that time, he will begin to feel and use his attainments in every way he wishes.

However, in truth, he did not add a thing to the attainments he had achieved in the beginning. It is rather like ripening: previously it was unripe, hence he could not understand it, and now its ripening has completed.

Thus, you see the big difference from the conducts of noetic phenomena. For this reason, the definitions we are accustomed to using will not suffice for us with noetic phenomena. We are compelled to use only the conducts that apply to corporeal matters, since their shapes are completely similar, although their substance is utterly remote.

FOUR LANGUAGES ARE USED IN THE WISDOM OF TRUTH

Four languages are used in the wisdom of truth:

1. The language of the Bible, its names, and appellations.

2. The language of laws. This language is very close to the language of the Bible.

3. The language of legends, which is very far from the Bible, since it has no consideration of reality. Strange names and appellations are attributed to this language, and also, it does not relate to concepts by way of root and its branch.

4. The language of Sefirot and Partzufim. In general, sages had a strong inclination to conceal it from the ignorant, since they believed that wisdom and ethics go hand in hand. Hence, the first sages hid

the wisdom in writing, using lines, dots, tops, and bottoms. This is how the alphabet was formed with the twenty-two letters before us.

The Language of the Bible

The language of the Bible is the primary, rudimentary language, perfectly suited for its task, as for the most part, it contains a root and branch relation. This is the easiest language to understand. This language is also the oldest; it is the Holy Tongue, attributed to *Adam HaRishon*.

This language has two advantages and one disadvantage. Its first advantage is that it is easy to understand, and even beginners in attainment immediately understand all they need. The second advantage is that it clarifies matters extensively and in depth, more than in all other languages.

Its disadvantage is that it cannot be used for discussing particular issues or connections of cause and consequence. This is so because every matter needs to be clarified in its fullest measure, as it is not self-evident in showing to which element it is referring, unless by presenting the whole matter. Hence, to emphasize the smallest detail, a complete story must be presented. This is why it is unfit for small details or for connections of cause and consequence.

Also, the language of prayers and blessings is taken from the language of the Bible.

The Language of Laws

The language of laws is not of reality, but of the existence of reality. This language is taken entirely from the language of the Bible according to the roots of the laws presented there. It has one advantage over the Bible: it greatly elaborates on every matter and hence points to the Upper Roots more accurately.

However, its great disadvantage, compared to the language of the Bible, is that it is very difficult to understand. This is the most difficult of all the languages, and only a complete sage, called "entering and exiting without harm," will attain it. Of course, it also contains the first disadvantage, as it is taken from the Bible.

THE LANGUAGE OF LEGENDS

The language of legends is easy to understand through the allegories that perfectly fit the desired meaning. In superficial examination, it seems even easier to understand than the language of the Bible. Yet, for complete understanding, it is a very difficult language, since it does not confine itself to speaking in sequences of root and branch, but only in allegories and marvelous wit. However, it is very rich in resolving abstruse and odd concepts that concern the essence of the degree in its state, for itself, which cannot be explained in the languages of Bible and law.

THE LANGUAGE OF KABBALISTS

The language of Kabbalists is a language in the full sense of the word: very precise, both concerning root and branch and concerning cause and consequence. It has a unique merit of being able to express subtle details in this language without any limits. Also, through it, it is possible to approach the desired matter directly, without the need to connect it with what precedes it or follows it.

However, despite all the sublime merits that you find in it, there is a great fault to it: it is very difficult to attain, almost impossible, except from a Kabbalist sage and from a wise one who understands with his own mind. This means that even one who understands the rest of the degrees from below Upwards and from Above downwards with his own mind, will still not understand a thing in this language until he receives it from a sage who had already received the language from his teacher face-to-face.

The Language of Kabbalah Is Contained in All

The names, appellations, and *Gematrias* belong entirely to the wisdom of Kabbalah. The reason they are found in the other languages, too, is that all the languages are included in the wisdom of Kabbalah. This is so because these are all particular cases that the other languages must be assisted with.

But one should not think that these four languages, which serve to explain the wisdom of Godly revelation, evolved one at a time, over time. The truth is that all four appeared before the sages simultaneously.

In truth, each consists of all the others. The language of Kabbalah exists in the Bible, such as the standing on the *Tzur* (rock), the thirteen attributes of mercy in the Torah and in *Micah*, and, to an extent, it is sensed in each and every verse. There are also the chariots in Isaiah and Ezekiel, and atop them all *The Song of Songs*, all of which is purely the language of Kabbalah. It is similar in laws and in legends, and all the more so with the matter of the unerasable names, which bear the same meaning in all the languages.

Order of the Evolution of the Languages

Within everything is a gradual development, and the easiest language to use is one whose development is completed before the others. Hence, the first products were in the language of the Bible, as it is the most convenient language and was prevalent at the time.

Following it came the language of laws, since it is completely immersed in the language of the Bible, as well as because it was needed in order to show the people how to implement the laws.

The third was the language of legends. Although it is found in many places in the Bible, too, it is only as an auxiliary language because its wit rushes the perception of matters. However, it cannot be used as a basic language, as it lacks the precision of root and its branch. Thus, it was rarely used and hence did not develop.

And even though legends were used extensively during the time of the Tanaaim and the Amoraim, it was only in conjunction with the language of the Bible, to open the words of our sages—Rabbi... started, etc., (and other suffixes). In truth, expansive use of this language by our sages began after the concealment of the language of Kabbalah, during the days of Yohanan Ben Zakai and soon before, meaning seventy years prior to the ruin of the Temple.

The last to evolve was the language of Kabbalah. This was so because of the difficulties in understanding it: in addition to attainment, one needs to understand the meaning of its words. Hence, even those who understood it could not use it, since, for the most part, they were alone in their generation and had no one with whom to study. Our sages called that language, *Maase Merkavah*, since it is a special language by which one can elaborate on the details of the *Herkev* (composition) of the degrees in one another, and not at all with any other.

The Language of Kabbalah Is Like any Spoken Language, and Its Preference Is in the Meaning Contained within a Single Word!

At first glance, the language of Kabbalah seems like a mixture of the three above-mentioned languages. However, one who understands how to use it will find that it is a unique language in and of itself from beginning to end. This does not pertain to the words, but to their meanings. This is the whole difference between them.

In the first three languages, there is almost no meaning to a single word, allowing the examiner to understand what the word implies. Only by joining a few words, and sometimes issues, can their content and meaning be understood. The advantage in the language of Kabbalah is that each and every word in it discloses its content and meaning to the examiner in utter precision, no less than in any other human tongue: each word carries its own precise definition and cannot be replaced with another.

Forgetting the Wisdom

Since the concealment of *The Zohar*, this important language has gradually been forgotten, as it was being used by fewer and fewer people. Also, there was a cessation of one generation, where the receiving sage did not convey it to an understanding receiver. Ever since then, there has been an immeasurable deficit.

You can evidently see that Kabbalist Rabbi Moshe de Leon, who was the last to possess it and by whom it appeared in the world, did not understand a word of it. This is because in those books where he introduces pieces of *The Book of Zohar*, it is clear that he did not understand the words at all, as he interpreted it according to the language of the Bible. He confused the understanding completely, although he himself had a wonderful attainment, as his compositions demonstrate.

So it was for generations: all the Kabbalists dedicated their entire lives to understanding the language of *The Zohar*, but could not find their hands and legs, since they forced the language of the Bible on it. For this reason, this book was sealed before them, as it was to Rabbi Moshe de Leon himself.

KABBALAH OF THE ARI

This was so until the arrival of the unique Kabbalist, the Ari. His attainment was above and beyond any boundary, and he opened the language of *The Zohar* for us and paved our way in it. Had he not passed away so young, it is hard to imagine the amount of Light that would be drawn out of *The Zohar*. The little we have been blessed with has paved a way and inlet, and true hope that over the generations our understanding would grow to fully grasp it.

Yet, you must understand the reason why all the great sages who followed the Ari abandoned all the books that they compiled in this wisdom and in the commentaries on *The Zohar*, and nearly prohibited themselves even from being seen, and dedicated their lives to the words of the Ari. This was not because they did not believe in the sanctity of the sages preceding the Ari; God forbid that we should think so. Anyone with eyes in the wisdom could see that the attainment of those great sages in the wisdom of truth was immeasurable. Only an ignorant fool could doubt them. However, their logic in the wisdom followed the first three languages.

Although each language is true and fitting in its place, it is not completely fitting, and quite misleading to understand the wisdom of Kabbalah contained in *The Zohar* using these orders. This is so because it is a completely different language, since it was forgotten. For this reason, we do not use their explanations, either the explanations of Rabbi Moshe de Leon himself, or his successors', as their words in interpreting *The Zohar* are not true, and to this day we have but one commentator—the Ari.

In light of the above, it follows that the internality of the wisdom of Kabbalah is none other than the internality of the Bible, the Talmud, and the legends. The only difference between them is in their explanations.

This is similar to a wisdom that has been translated into four languages. Naturally, the essence of the wisdom has not changed at all by the change of language. All we need to think of is which translation is the most convenient for conveying the wisdom to the student.

So is the matter before us: the wisdom of truth, meaning the wisdom of the revelation of Godliness in His Ways to the creatures, like secular teachings, must be passed on from generation to generation. Each generation adds a link to its former, and thus the wisdom evolves. Moreover, it becomes more suitable for expansion in the public.

Hence, each sage must pass on to his students and to the following generations everything he has inherited in the wisdom from earlier generations, as well as the additions he himself has been rewarded with. Clearly, the spiritual attainment—as it is attained by the attaining—cannot be passed on to another, and all the more so be written in a book. This is so because spiritual objects cannot come in letters of the imagination whatsoever (and even though it is written, "...and by the ministry of the prophets have I used similitudes," it is not literally so).

ORDER OF PASSING THE WISDOM

Thus, how can one who attains convey one's attainments to the generations and to students? Know that there is only one way for this: the way of root and branch. All the worlds and everything that fills them, in their every detail, emerged from the Creator in One, Unique, and Unified Thought. And the Thought alone cascaded and created all the many worlds and creations and their conducts, as explained in *The Tree of Life* and in the *Tikkuney Zohar*.

Hence, they are all equal to one another, like seal and imprint, where the first seal is imprinted in all. As a result, we call the closer worlds to the Thought about the purpose, "roots," and the farther worlds from the purpose we call "branches." This is so because the end of the act is in the preliminary thought.

Now we can understand the common idiom in the legends of our sages: "and watches it from the end of the world to its end." Should they not have said, "...from the beginning of the world to its end"? But there are two ends: an end according to the **distance from the purpose**, meaning the last branches in this world, and 2) an end called "**the final purpose**," since the purpose is revealed at the end of the matter.

But as we have explained, "The end of the act is in the preliminary thought." Hence, we find the purpose at the beginning of the worlds. This is what we refer to as "**the first world**," or "**the first seal**." All other worlds stem from it, and this is why all creations—still, vegetative, animate, and speaking—in all their incidents exist in their fullest form right at the first world. And what does not exist there cannot appear in the world, since one does not give what one does not have.

ROOT AND BRANCH IN THE WORLDS

Now it is easy to understand the matter of roots and branches in the worlds. Each of the manifold still, vegetative, animate, and speaking in this world have their corresponding parts in the world Above it, without any difference in their form, but only in their substance. Thus, an animal or a rock in this world is a corporeal matter, and its corresponding animal or rock in the Higher World is a spiritual matter, occupying no place or time. However, their quality is the same.

And here we should certainly add the matter of relation between matter and form, which is naturally conditioned on the quality of form, too. Similarly, with the majority of the still, vegetative, animate, and speaking in the Upper World, you will find their similitude and likeness in the world Above the Upper. This continues through the first world, where all the elements are completed, as it is written, "And God saw every thing that He had made, and, behold, it was very good."

This is why the Kabbalists wrote that the world is at the center of everything, to indicate the above, that the **end of the act** is the first world, meaning **the goal**. Also, the remoteness from the goal is called "the descent of the worlds from their Emanator" down to this corporeal world, the farthest from the purpose.

However, the end of all the corporeals is to gradually develop and achieve the goal that the Creator had designed for them, meaning the first world. Compared to this world, which we are in, it is the last world, meaning of the end of the matter. This is why it seems that the world of the goal is the last world, and that we, people of this world, are in between them.

ESSENCE OF THE WISDOM OF TRUTH

Now it is clear that as the emergence of the living species in this world and the conduct of their lives are a wondrous wisdom, the appearance of the Divine Abundance in the world, the degrees and the conduct of their actions unite to create a wondrous wisdom, far more than the science of physics. This is so because physics is mere knowledge of the arrangements of a particular kind existing in a particular world. It is unique to its subject, and no other wisdom is included in it.

This is not so with the wisdom of truth, since it is knowledge of the whole of the still, vegetative, animate, and speaking in all the worlds with all their instances and conducts, as they were included in the Creator's Thought, that is, in the purpose. For this reason, all the teachings in the world, from the least of them unto the greatest of them, are wondrously included in it, as it equalizes all the different teachings, the most different and the most remote from one another, as the east from the west. It makes them all equal, meaning the orders of each teaching are compelled to come by its ways.

For example, the science of physics is arranged precisely by the order of the worlds and the *Sefirot*. Similarly, the science of astronomy is arranged by that same order, and so is the science of music, etc. Thus, we find in it that all the teachings are arranged and follow a single connection and a single relation, and they are all like the relation of the child to its progenitor. Hence, they condition one another; that is, the wisdom of truth is conditioned by all the teachings, and all the teachings are conditioned by it. This is why we do not find a single genuine Kabbalist without comprehensive knowledge in all the teachings of the world, since they acquire them from the wisdom of truth itself, as they are included in it.

Unity

The greatest wonder about this wisdom is the integration in it: all the elements of the vast reality are incorporated in it, until they come into a single thing—the Almighty, and all of them together.

In the beginning, you find that all the teachings in the world are reflected in it. They are arranged within it precisely by its own orders. Subsequently, we find that all the worlds and the orders in the wisdom of truth itself, which are immeasurable, unite under only ten realities, called "Ten *Sefirot*."

Afterwards, these ten *Sefirot* arrange in four manners, which are the four-letter Name. After that, these four manners are included in the tip of the *Yod*, which implies the *Ein Sof* (Infinity).

In this way, one who begins in the wisdom must begin with the tip of the *Yod*, and from there to the ten *Sefirot* in the first world, called "the world of *Adam Kadmon*." From there one sees how the numerous details in the world of *Adam Kadmon* necessarily extend by way of cause and consequence, by the same laws we find in astronomy and physics, meaning constant, unbreakable laws that necessarily stem from one another, cascading from one another, from the tip of the *Yod* down to all the elements in the world of *Adam Kadmon*. From there they are imprinted by one another from the four worlds by way of seal and imprint, until we arrive at all the elements in this world. Afterwards, they are reintegrated in one another until they all come to the world of *Adam Kadmon*, then to the ten *Sefirot*, then to the four-letter Name, up to the tip of the *Yod*.

We could ask, "If the material is unknown, how can we study and scrutinize it"? Indeed, such as that you will find in all the teachings. For example, when studying anatomy—the various organs and how they affect one another—these organs have no similarity to the general subject, which is the whole, living human being. However, over time, when you thoroughly know the wisdom, you can establish a general relation of all the details upon which the body is conditioned.

So it is here: the general topic is the revelation of Godliness to His creations, by way of the purpose, as it is written, "...for the earth shall be full of the knowledge of the Lord." However, a novice will certainly have no knowledge of the general topic, which is conditioned by all of them. For this reason, one must acquire all the details and how they affect each other, as well as their causes by way of cause and consequence, until one completes the whole wisdom. And when one thoroughly knows everything, if he has a purified soul, it is certain that he will ultimately be rewarded with the general topic.

And even if he is not rewarded, it is still a great reward to acquire any perception of this great wisdom, whose advantage over all other teachings is as the value of their topics, and as the advantage of the Creator over His creations is valued. Similarly, this wisdom, whose subject is Him, is far more valuable than the wisdom whose subject is His creatures.

It is not because it is imperceptible that the world refrains from contemplating it. After all, an astronomer has no perception of the stars and the planets, but only of their movements, which they perform with wondrous wisdom that is predetermined in wondrous Providence. Similarly, the knowledge in the wisdom of truth is not more hidden than that, as even beginners thoroughly understand the movements. Rather, the whole prevention was because Kabbalists very wisely hid it from the world.

GIVING PERMISSION

I am glad that I have been born in such a generation when it is permitted to disclose the wisdom of truth. And should you ask, "How do I know that it is permitted?" I will reply that I have been given permission to disclose. Until now, the ways by which it is possible to publicly engage and to fully explain each word have not been revealed to any sage. And I, too, have sworn by my teacher not to disclose, as did all the students before me. However, this oath and this prohibition apply only to those manners that are given orally from generation to generation, back to the prophets and before. Had these ways been revealed to the public, they would cause much harm, for reasons known only to us.

Yet, the way in which I engage in my books is a permitted way. Moreover, I have been instructed by my teacher to expand it as much as I can. We call it "the manner of clothing the matters." You will see in the writings of Rashbi that he calls this way, "giving permission," and this is what the Creator has given me to the fullest extent. We deem it as dependent not on the greatness of the sage, but on the state of the generation, as our sages said, "Little Samuel was worthy, etc., but his generation was unworthy."

This is why I said that my being rewarded with the manner of disclosing the wisdom is because of my generation.

ABSTRACT NAMES

It is a grave mistake to think that the language of Kabbalah uses abstract names. On the contrary, it touches only upon the actual. Indeed, there are things in the world that are real even though we have no perception of them, such as the magnet and electricity. Yet, who would be so foolish as to say that these are abstract names? After all, we thoroughly know their actions, and we could not care less that we do not know their essence. In the end, we refer to them as sure subjects to the actions that relate to them. And this is a real name. Even an infant who is just learning to speak can name them, if he only begins to feel their actions. This is our law: **All that we do not attain, we do not name.**

ESSENCE IS NOT PERCEIVED IN THE CORPOREALS

Moreover, even the things we imagine we attain by their essence, such as rocks and trees, after honest examination we are left with zero attainment in their essence, since we only attain their actions, which occur in conjunction with the encounter of our senses with them.

SOUL

For example, when Kabbalah states that there are three forces, 1) Body, 2) Animate Soul, and 3) Sacred Soul, this does not refer to the essence of the soul. The essence of the soul is fluid; it is what psychologists refer to as "self" and materialists as "electric."[5]

---

5   Rav Laitman explains that by "electric," Baal HaSulam means based on atoms.

It is a waste of time to speak of its essence, as it is not arranged for impression through the touch of our senses, as with all corporeal objects. However, by observing in the essence of this fluid three kinds of actions in the spiritual worlds, we thoroughly distinguish between them by different names, according to their actual operations in the Upper Worlds. Thus, there are no abstract names here, but rather tangible ones in the full sense of the word.

ADVANTAGE OF MY COMMENTARY OVER PREVIOUS COMMENTARIES

We can be assisted by secular teachings in interpreting matters in the wisdom of Kabbalah, since the wisdom of Kabbalah is the root of everything and they are all included in it. Some were assisted by anatomy, such as in, "then without my flesh shall I see God," and some were assisted by philosophy. Latterly, there is extensive use of the wisdom of psychology. But all these are not considered true commentaries, since they do not interpret anything in the wisdom of Kabbalah itself, only show us how the rest of the teachings are included in it. This is why the observers cannot be assisted by one place, in another place. ...even though the wisdom of serving God is the closest wisdom to Kabbalah from all the external teachings.

And needless to say, it is impossible to be assisted by interpretations according to the science of anatomy, or by philosophy. For this reason, I said that I am the first interpreter by root and branch, and cause and consequence. Hence, if one were to understand some matter through my commentary, one can be certain that everywhere this matter appears in *The Zohar* and in the *Tikkunim*, he can be assisted by it, as with the commentaries on the literal, where you can be assisted by one place for all the other places.

The style of interpreting according to external teachings is a waste of time because it is nothing more than a testimony to the genuineness of one over the other. And an external teaching needs no testimony, as Providence has prepared five senses to testify for it, and in Kabbalah (nevertheless) one should understand the argument prior to bringing testimony to the argument.

STYLE OF INTERPRETING ACCORDING TO EXTERNAL TEACHINGS

This is the source of Rav Shem Tov's mistake: he interpreted *The Guide for the Perplexed* according to the wisdom of Kabbalah, and he did not know, or pretended not to know, that the wisdom of medicine, or any other wisdom, could be interpreted according to the wisdom of Kabbalah no less than the wisdom of philosophy. This is so because all the teachings are included in it and were imprinted by its seal.

Of course, the *Guide to the Perplexed* did not refer at all to what Rav Shem Tov interpreted, and he did not see how... in *The Book of Creation*, he interpreted the Kabbalah according to philosophy. I have already proven that such a style of commentaries is a waste of time, since external teachings need no testimony, and it is pointless to bring testimony to the truthfulness of the wisdom of Kabbalah before its words are interpreted.

It is like a prosecutor who brings witnesses to verify his words before he has explained his arguments (except for books that deal with the work of God, since the wisdom of serving God truly needs witnesses to its truthfulness and success, and we should be assisted by the wisdom of truth).

However, all the compositions of this style are not at all a waste. After we thoroughly understand the wisdom in itself, we will be able to receive much assistance from analogies, how all the teachings are included in it, as well as the manners by which to seek them.

ATTAINING THE WISDOM

There are three orders in the wisdom of truth:

1. The originality in the wisdom. It requires no human assistance, as it is entirely the gift of God, and no stranger shall interfere with it.

2. The understanding of the sources that one has attained from Above. It is like a person who sees that the whole world is set before his eyes, and yet he must exert and study to understand this world. Although he sees everything with his own eyes, there are fools and there are wise. This understanding is called "the wisdom of truth," and *Adam HaRishon* was the first to receive a sequence of sufficient knowledge by which to understand and to successfully maximize everything he saw and attained with his eyes.

    The order of this knowledge is given only from mouth to mouth. And there is also an order of evolution in them, where each can add to his friend or regress (whereas in the first discernment everyone receives equally without adding or subtracting, like Adam, in understanding the reality of this world. In viewing it, all are equal, but this is not so in understanding it—some evolve from generation to generation and some regress). And the order of its conveyance is sometimes called "conveying the Explicit Name," and it is given under many conditions, but only in words, not in writing.

3. This is a written order. It is a completely new thing, since besides containing much room for the

development of the wisdom, through which each inherits all the expansions of his attainments to the following generations, there is another magnificent power in it: All who engage in it, although they still do not understand what is written in it, are purified by it, and the Upper Lights draw closer to them. And this order contains four languages, as we have explained above, and the language of Kabbalah exceeds them all.

Order of Conveying the Wisdom

The most successful way for one who wishes to learn the wisdom is to search for a genuine Kabbalist and follow all his instructions, until one is rewarded with understanding the wisdom in one's own mind, meaning the first discernment. Afterwards, one will be rewarded with its conveyance mouth to mouth, which is the second discernment, and after that, understand in writing, which is the third discernment. Then, one will have inherited all the wisdom and its instruments from his teacher with ease, and will be left with all one's time to develop and expand.

However, in reality there is a second way: through one's great yearning, the sights of the Heavens will open for him and he will attain all the origins by himself. This is the first discernment. Yet, afterwards one must still labor and exert extensively, until one finds a Kabbalist sage before whom one can bow and obey, and from whom to receive the wisdom by way of conveyance face to face, which is the second discernment, and then the third discernment.

And since one is not attached to a Kabbalist sage from the outset, the attainments come with great efforts and consume much time, leaving one with only little time to develop in it. Also, sometimes the knowledge comes after the fact, as it is written, "and they shall die without wisdom." These are ninety-nine percent and what we call, "entering but not exiting." They are as fools and ignorant in this world, who see the world set before them but do not understand any of it, except the bread in their mouths.

Indeed, in the first way, too, not everyone succeeds. This is because the majority, having attained, become complacent and stop subjugating themselves to their teacher sufficiently, as they are not worthy of the conveyance of the wisdom. In this case, the sage must hide the essence of the wisdom from them, and "they shall die without wisdom," "entering but not exiting."

This is so because there are harsh and strict conditions in conveying the wisdom, which stem from necessary reasons. Hence, very few are regarded highly enough by their teachers for them to find them worthy of this thing, and happy are the rewarded.

The Wisdom of Kabbalah and Philosophy

What Is Spirituality?

Philosophy has gone through a great deal of trouble to prove that corporeality is the offspring of spirituality and that the soul begets the body. Still, their words are unacceptable to the heart in any manner. Their primary mistake is their erroneous perception of spirituality: they determined that spirituality fathered corporeality, which is certainly a fib.

Any parent must somehow resemble its progeny. This relation is the path and the route by which its sequel extends. In addition, every operator must have some regard to its operation by which to contact it. Since you say that spirituality is denied of any corporeal incidents, then such a path does not exist, or a relation by which the spiritual can contact and set it into any kind of motion.

However, understanding the meaning of the word, "spirituality," has nothing to do with philosophy. This is because how can they discuss something that they have never seen or felt? What do their rudiments stand on?

If there is any definition that can tell spiritual from corporeal, it belongs only to those who have attained a spiritual thing and felt it. These are the genuine Kabbalists; thus, it is the wisdom of Kabbalah that we need.

PHILOSOPHY WITH REGARD TO HIS ESSENCE

Philosophy loves to concern itself with His Essence and prove which rules do not apply to Him. However, Kabbalah has no dealings whatsoever with it, for how can the unattainable and imperceptible be defined? Indeed, a negative definition is just as valid as a positive definition. For if you see an object from a distance and recognize its negatives, meaning all that it is not, that, too, is considered seeing and some extent of recognition. If an object is truly out of sight, even its negative characteristics are not apparent.

If, for example, we see a black image from a distance, but can still determine that it is neither human nor bird, it is considered vision. If it had been even farther still, we would have been unable to determine that it is not a person.

This is the origin of their confusion and invalidity. Philosophy loves to pride itself on understanding all the negatives about His essence. However, the sages of Kabbalah put their hand to their mouth at this point, and do not give Him even a simple name, **for we do not define by name or word that which we do not attain.** That is because a word designates some degree of attainment. However, Kabbalists do speak a great deal about His illumination in reality, meaning all those illuminations they have actually attained, as validly as tangible attainment.

THE SPIRITUAL IS A FORCE WITHOUT A BODY

That is what Kabbalists define as "spirituality" and that is what they talk about. It has no image or space or time or any corporeal value (In my opinion, philosophy has generally worn a mantle that is not its own, for it has pilfered definitions from the wisdom of Kabbalah, and made delicacies with human understanding. Had it not been for that, they would never have thought of fabricating such acumen.) However, it is only a potential force, meaning not a force that is clothed in an ordinary, worldly body, but a force without a body.

A Spiritual Vessel Is Called "A Force"

This is the place to point out that the force that spirituality speaks of does not refer to the spiritual Light itself. That spiritual Light extends directly from His essence and is therefore the same as His Essence. This means that we have no perception or attainment in the spiritual Light that we may define by name. Even the name, "Light," is borrowed and is not real. Thus, we must know that the name, "Force," without a body refers specifically to the "spiritual vessel."

Lights and Vessels

Therefore, we must not inquire how the sages of the Kabbalah, which fill the entire wisdom with their insights, differentiate between the various Lights. That is because these observations do not refer to the Lights themselves, but to the impression of the vessel, being the above-mentioned force, which is affected by its encounter with the Light.

Vessels and Lights (the meaning of the words)

Here is where the line between the gift and the love that it creates must be drawn. The Lights, meaning the impression on the vessel, which is attainable, is called "form and matter together." The impression is the form and the above force is the matter.

However, the love that is created is considered a **"form without matter."** This means that if we separate the love from the gift itself,

185

as though it never clothed any gift, but only in the abstract name, "the love of God," then it is regarded as a form. In that event, the practice of it is regarded as "**Formative Kabbalah.**" However, it would still be regarded as real, without any similarity to Formative Philosophy, since the spirit of this love remains in the attainment, completely separated from the gift, being the Light itself.

MATTER AND FORM IN KABBALAH

The reason is that although this love is merely a consequence of the gift, it is still far more important than the gift itself. It is like a great king who gives an unimportant object to a person. Although the gift itself is worthless, the love and the attention of the king make it priceless and precious. Thus, it is completely separated from the matter, being the Light and the gift, in a way that the work and the distinction remain carved in the attainment with only the love itself, while the gift is seemingly forgotten from the heart. Therefore, this aspect of the wisdom is called the "**Formative Wisdom of Kabbalah.**" Indeed, this part is the most important part of the wisdom.

ABYA

This love consists of four parts that are much like human love: when we first receive the present, we still do not refer to the giver of the gift as one who loves us, all the more so if the giver of the present is important and the receiver is not equal to him.

However, the repetitive giving and the perseverance will make even the most important person seem like a true, equal lover. This is because the law of love does not apply between great and small, as two real lovers must feel equal.

Thus, you can measure four degrees of love here. The incident is called **Assiya**, the repetition of the giving of gifts is called **Yetzira**, and the appearance of the love itself is called **Beria**.

It is here that the study of the **Formative Wisdom of Kabbalah** begins, for it is in this degree that love is separated from the presents. This is the meaning of, "and create darkness," meaning the Light is removed from the *Yetzira* and the love remains without Light, without its gifts.

Then comes **Atzilut**. After it has tasted and entirely separated the form from the matter, as in, "and create darkness," it became worthy of ascending to the degree of *Atzilut*, where the form clothes the substance once more, meaning Light and love together.

THE ORIGIN OF THE SOUL

Everything spiritual is perceived as a separated force from the body because it has no corporeal image. However, because of that, it remains isolated and completely separated from the corporeal. In such a state, how can it set anything corporeal in motion, much less beget anything physical, when it has no relation by which to come in contact with the physical?

THE ACIDIC ELEMENT

However, the truth is that the force itself is also considered a genuine matter, just as any corporeal matter in the concrete world, and the fact that it has no image that the human senses can perceive does not reduce the value of the substance, which is the "force."

Take a molecule of oxygen as an example: It is a constituent of most materials in the world. Yet, if you take a bottle with pure oxygen when it is not mixed with any other substance, you will find that it seems as though the bottle is completely empty. You will not be able to notice anything about it; it will be completely like air, intangible and invisible to the eye.

If we remove the lid and smell it, we will find no scent; if we taste it, we will find no flavor, and if we put it on a scale, it will not weigh more than the empty bottle. The same applies to hydrogen, which is also tasteless, scentless, and weightless.

However, when putting these two elements together, they will immediately become a liquid—drinking water that possesses both taste and weight. If we put the water inside active lime, it will immediately mix with it and become as solid as the lime itself.

Thus, the elements, oxygen and hydrogen, in which there is no tangible perception whatsoever, become a solid body. Therefore, how can we determine about natural forces that they are not a corporeal substance just because they are not arranged in such a way that our senses can perceive them? Moreover, we can evidently see that most of the tangible materials in our world consist preliminarily of the element of oxygen, which human senses cannot perceive and feel!

Moreover, even in the tangible reality, the solid and the liquid that we can vividly perceive in our tangible world might turn to air and fume at a certain temperature. Likewise, the vapors may turn to solids when the temperature drops.

In that event, we should wonder, **how does one give that which one does not possess?** We clearly see that all the tangible images come from elements that are in and of themselves intangible, and do not exist as materials in and of themselves. Likewise, all the fixed pictures that we know and use to define materials are inconsistent and do not exist in their own right. Rather, they only dress and undress forms under the influence of conditions such as heat or cold.

The primary part of the corporeal substance is the "force" in it, though we are not yet able to tell these forces apart, as with chemical elements. Perhaps in the future they will be discovered in their pure form, as we have only recently discovered the chemical elements.

EQUAL FORCE IN SPIRITUAL AND PHYSICAL

In a word: all the names that we ascribe materials are completely fabricated, meaning stem from our concrete perception in our five senses. They do not exist in and of themselves. On the other hand, any definition we ascribe to the force, which separates it from the material, is also fabricated. Even when science reaches its ultimate development, we will still have to regard only the tangible reality. This means that within any material operation we see and feel, we must perceive its operator, who is also a substance, like the operation itself. There is a correlation between them, or they would not have come to it.

We must know that this erring of separating the operator from the operation comes from the **Formative Philosophy**, which insisted on proving that the spiritual act influences the corporeal operation. That resulted in erroneous assumptions such as the above, for which Kabbalah has no need.

BODY AND SOUL IN THE UPPER ONES

The opinion of Kabbalah in this matter is crystal clear, excluding any mixture of philosophy. This is because in the minds of Kabbalists, even the spiritual, separated, conceptual entities, which philosophy denies having any corporeality and displays them as purely conceptual substance, although they are indeed spiritual, more sublime and abstract, they still consist of a **body and soul,** just like the physical human.

Therefore, you need not wonder how two can win the prize and say that they are complex. Furthermore, philosophy believes that anything complex will eventually disintegrate and decompose, meaning die. Thus, how can one declare that they are both complex *and* eternal?

Lights and Vessels

Indeed, their thoughts are not our thoughts, for the way of the sages of the Kabbalah is one of finding actual proof of attainment, making its revocation through intellectual pondering impossible. But let me make these matters so that they are clear for every person's understanding.

First, we must know that the difference between Lights and vessels is created immediately in the first emanated being from *Ein Sof* (Infinity). Naturally, the first emanation is also the most complete and purer than everything that follows it. It is certain that it receives this pleasantness and completeness from His Essence, which wishes to grant it every pleasantness and pleasure.

It is known that the measurement of the pleasure is essentially the will to receive it. That is because what we most want to receive feels as the most pleasurable. Because of that, we should discern two observations in this first emanation: the "will to receive" that received Essence, and the received Essence itself.

We should also know that the will to receive is what we perceive as the "body" of the emanated, meaning its primary essence, being the vessel to receive His goodness. The second is the Essence of the good that is received, which is His Light, which is eternally extended to the emanation.

It follows that we necessarily distinguish two discernments that clothe one another even in the most sublime spiritual that the heart can conceive. It is the opposite of the opinion of philosophy, which fabricated that the separated entities are not complex materials. It is necessary that that "will to receive," which necessarily exists in the emanated (for without it there would be no pleasure but coercion, and no feeling of pleasure) is absent in His Essence. This is the reason for the name "emanated," since it is no longer His Essence, for from whom would He receive?

However, the bounty that it receives is necessarily a part of His Essence, for here there need not be any innovation. Thus, we see the great difference between the generated body and the received abundance, which is deemed His essence.

How Can a Spiritual Beget a Corporeal?

It is seemingly difficult to understand how the spiritual can beget and extend anything corporeal. This question is an ancient philosophical query that much ink has been spilt attempting to resolve.

The truth is that this question is a difficult one only if one follows their doctrine. That is because they have determined the form of spirituality without any connection to anything corporeal. That produces a difficult question: how can the spiritual lead to or father anything corporeal?

But it is the view of the sages of Kabbalah that this is not difficult at all, for their terms are the complete opposite to those of philosophers. They maintain that any spiritual quality equalizes with the corporeal quality like two drops in a pond. Thus, the relationships are of the utmost affinity and there is no separation between them, except in the substance: the spiritual consists of a spiritual substance and the corporeal consists of a corporeal substance.

However, all the qualities in spiritual materials abide in corporeal materials, too, as explained in the article, "The Essence of the Wisdom of Kabbalah."

The old philosophy presents three opinions as obstacles before my explanation: The first is their decision that the power of the human intellect is the eternal soul, man's essence. The second is their conjecture that the body is an upshot of the soul. The third is their saying that spiritual entities are simple objects and not complex.

Materialistic Psychology

Not only is it the wrong place to argue with them about their fabricated conjectures, but also the time of supporters of such views has already passed and their authority revoked. We should also thank the experts of materialistic psychology for that, which built its plinth on the ruin of the former, winning the public's favor. Now everyone admits to the nullity of philosophy, for it is not built on concrete foundations.

This old doctrine became a stumbling rock and a deadly thorn to the sages of Kabbalah because where they should have subdued before the sages of Kabbalah, and assume abstinence and prudence, sanctity, and purity before the sages disclosed before them even the smallest thing in spirituality, they easily received what they had wanted from the formative philosophy. Without payment or price, they watered them from their fountain of wisdom to satiation, and refrained from delving in the wisdom of Kabbalah until the wisdom has almost been forgotten from among Israel. Hence, we are grateful to materialistic psychology for handing it a deadly blow.

I Am Solomon

The above is much like a fable that our sages tell: Asmodeus (the devil) drove King Solomon four hundred parsas (a distant measurement) from Jerusalem and left Him with no money and means of sustenance. Then he sat in King Solomon's throne while the king was begging at the doors. Every place he went, he said: "I am Ecclesiastes!" but none believed him. And so he went from town to town declaring, "I am Solomon!" But when he came to the Sanhedrin (the sages of the Talmud) they said: "A fool does not utter the same folly all the time, saying, 'I was once a king.'"

It seems as though the name is not the essence of a person, but rather the owner of the name is. Therefore, how can a wise man such as Solomon not be recognized if he is indeed the owner of the name? Moreover, it is the person that dignifies the name and he should display his wisdom!

THREE PREVENTIONS

There are three reasons that prevent us from knowing the owner of a name:

1. Because of its truthfulness, the wisdom becomes clear only when all its details appear together. Therefore, before one knows the whole wisdom, it is impossible to see even a fraction of it. Thus, it is the publicity of its truthfulness that we need, so as to have enough prior faith in it to make a great effort.

2. Just as Asmodeus, the demon, wore the clothes of King Solomon and inherited his throne, philosophy sat on the throne of Kabbalah with easier concepts to grasp, for the lie is quickly accepted. Therefore, there is a twofold trouble here: first, the wisdom of truth is profound and laborious, while philosophy is false and easily grasped; and second, it is superfluous, because philosophy is quite satisfying.

3. As the demon claims that King Solomon is mad, philosophy mocks and dismisses Kabbalah.

However, as long as wisdom is sublime, it is elevated above the people and separated from it. Because he was the wisest man, he was also higher than every man. Thus, the finest scholars could not understand him, except those friends, meaning the Sanhedrin, whom he taught his wisdom to every day for days and years. They are the ones who understood him and publicized his name in the entire world.

The reason for it is that minute wisdom is perceived in five minutes, and is thus attainable by anyone and can be easily publicized. However, a weighty concept will not be understood in less than several hours. It may even take days or years, depending on the intelligence. Accordingly, the greatest scholars will be understood only by a selected few in the generation, because profound concepts are founded on much prior knowledge.

It is therefore not surprising that the wisest of all men, who was exiled to a place where he was not known, could not demonstrate his wisdom or even show a hint of his wisdom before they believed that he was the owner of the name.

It is the same with the wisdom of Kabbalah in our time: the troubles and the exile that have come upon us brought us to forget it (and if there are people who do practice it, it is not in its favor, but rather harms it, for they did not receive it from a Kabbalist sage). Hence, in this generation, it is as King Solomon was in exile, declaring, "I am the wisdom, and all the flavors of religion and Torah are in me," yet none believe it.

But this is perplexing, for if it is a genuine wisdom, can it not display itself like all other wisdoms? It cannot. As King Solomon could not display his wisdom to the scholars at the place of his exile and had to come to Jerusalem, the place of the Sanhedrin, who studied and knew King Solomon, and testified to the depth of his wisdom, so it is with the wisdom of Kabbalah: it requires great sages who examine their hearts to study it for twenty or thirty years. Only then will they be able to testify to it.

And as King Solomon could not prevent Asmodeus from sitting on his throne, pretending to be him until he arrived in

Jerusalem, sages of Kabbalah observe philosophic theology and complain that they have stolen the upper shell of their wisdom, which Plato and his Greek predecessors had acquired while studying with the disciples of the prophets in Israel. They have stolen basic elements from the wisdom of Israel and wore a cloak that is not their own. To this day, philosophic theology sits on the throne of Kabbalah, being the hair under her mistress.

And who would believe the sages of Kabbalah while others sit on their throne? It is as when they did not believe King Solomon in exile, for they knew him to be sitting on his throne, meaning the demon, Asmodeus. As with King Solomon, it is hopeless that the truth will be exposed, for the wisdom is deep and cannot be revealed by testimony or by experimentation except to those believers that dedicate themselves to it with heart and soul.

Just as the Sanhedrin did not recognize King Solomon as long as the falsehood of Asmodeus did not appear, Kabbalah cannot prove its nature and truthfulness, and no revelations will suffice for the world to know it before the futility and falsehood of theological philosophy that has taken its throne becomes apparent.

Therefore, there was no such salvation for Israel as when the materialistic psychology appeared and struck theological philosophy on its head a lethal blow. Now, every person who seeks the Lord must bring Kabbalah back to its throne, and restore its past glory.

The Quality of the Wisdom of the Hidden in General

There are two parts in any understanding (recognition of reason). The first is in material elements, meaning the nature of the objects in the reality before us. The second is in the figurative elements devoid of those objects, meaning forms of mind and reason itself.

We shall call the first, "material learning," which is empirical, and is called "physics" ... and we shall call the second one, "figurative learning," which is theoretical, and is called "logic."

MATERIAL LEARNING IS ALSO DIVIDED INTO TWO, WHICH ARE FOUR

Sometimes we can minimize it into speaking of what is above nature. This is called "the wisdom of what is beyond nature," meaning according to specific subjects of the superior mind.

There are four parts here:

1. Material learning from the part called, "Nature's Law," which is empirical;

2. Material learning from the part called, "Nature's Law," which is the wisdom of what is beyond nature;

3. Material learning from the part called, "ancient," which is empirical and practical;

4. Material learning from the part called, "ancient," which is only the wisdom of what is beyond nature.

FIGURATIVE LEARNING

Figurative learning is one whose predicate is the Upper One. In material learning, the predicates are the degrees called "worlds" and *Partzufim*.

And yet, it is empirical and practical. Clearly, the superior principle in the wisdom of the hidden does not become any clearer now because it requires complete study in and of itself, and I have already shown that it is the revelation of His Godliness to His creatures, as explained in the essay, "The Essence of the Wisdom of Kabbalah," as I have elaborated there. Once you understand that, you will understand my explanation of the quality of the wisdom in general.

This Superior Principle Is Defined as One Unique, and Unified

One: It is obvious that the Upper One is one. He comprises the whole of reality, and all the times—past, present, and future—for one cannot give that which one does not have. Had the whole of reality and the existence of reality not been included in Him, they would not have emerged from Him, as is evident to scrutinizer, and without minding that we find corruptions in the manners of existence of reality.

Indeed, know that this is the study that the sages of the hidden call, "one." The first to study it was Abraham the Patriarch. (This is explained in the *Book of Creation* and is therefore attributed to Abraham the Patriarch.) This means that there aren't two authorities here—good and bad—but only good.

Unique: This indicates that He is still united and does not change because we feel the bad, not even in the relation between Him and His creations. For example, when a sick person comes to a physician to pull out a thorn, the physician who pulls it out hurts the patient. This is not considered that he has now changed and is doing harm. Rather, the physician and the patient, who loved one another before, are still loving even during the painful cutting. This is called "unique."

Unified: This indicates that His attitude toward creation, as a Creator, is only to disclose His uniqueness, for all the pleasantness, all the wisdom, and all the *Dvekut* (Adhesion) are expressed in this unification.

Material Learning and Empiric One

Material learning is to know the approach of the whole of reality of people, and their manners of existence, and manners of their development, from the first cause through their arrival in this world, both from above downward and from below upward. The main thing to know about them is the cause and consequence that applies to them, for this is the picture of every wisdom, like nature's law and the law of life.

Practical Learning

It is the nature of those degrees that one who attains finds in them tremendous pleasure and delight. This extends literally from one's coming by the will of the Upper One, since the ways of

His guidance over the existence of the world are by no more than two equal forces, where one who desires their work, draws them by enjoying during the work, and that pleasure compels them to it. When not wanting them to work, one repels them through suffering, when the creature suffers during the work and therefore leaves it.

This law is observed in full by animals and humans, as it serves the purpose. For this reason, its guidance becomes complicated and must change every single moment. Sometimes, the law is denied through the law of habit that becomes second nature for it.

The Nature of the Degrees

The nature of the degrees to the attaining is as the nature of animals. That is, the law of reward and punishment is observed strictly and inexorably, and even habit will not change it.

Two Parts to Material Studies

There are two parts to material studies: 1) reality; 2) their existence—the quantity and quality of their sustenance, and how they are attained: by whom and by what. For this reason, there is a very bitter taste in the spaces between each two degrees, and those who attain them loathe them vehemently. It is made and drawn upon them so they will not remain there in the middle, as is the case with simple animals. However, sometimes the attaining turn back when they remember the great delight that is there.

Klipa (Shell/Peel): No Turning Back in Spirituality

When they return, it is already a different degree, and is called *Klipa* (shell/peel) in relation to the initial degree.

Two Parts to Practical Learning

There are two parts to practical learning: the first sanctity; the second is *Klipa*. Sometimes, for some reason, sages, too, return to the place where there is the taste of a great delight in order to do something. However, they promptly leave it and resume their place. For this reason, the return is also called "sanctity."

And yet, for the most part, only the frightened and those of weak desire return there, wishing to avoid passing through the bitter path between the degrees, so they remain stuck there because they cannot rise to their aspired height.

The Manner of Work in the Names

The manner of work in the names is extension of much pleasantness. At that time one can draw that spirit in one's friend, as well, who is very inspired. By that he can heal him or command him and force him to do his will.

2. Practical Kabbalah

The Loss in Every Proliferation

We have explained above, concerning practical learning, that the Creator compels the creature through the light of pleasure in the work that dresses in him. What the Creator does not want, He prevents through the light of suffering that dresses in him. This is the meaning of the loss in every proliferation. "The more possessions, the more worry," etc., since there is a limit to every will of the Creator, as He desires many works up the ladder of development. Were there no limit to every pleasure, the creature would have become immersed in one work for the rest of one's life, and would not have climbed up the degrees.

For this reason, Providence limits him by pain that results from any excessive pleasure.

Beastly Repayment and Human Repayment

There is immediate pleasure, in which there is no issue of hope, but is rather repaid instantaneously, and then there is remote, anticipated pleasure, whose repayment is aspired for at a later date. The former is called "Sensual Repayment," and the second is the "Intellectual" one. The first applies to all living beings, and its conduct is sustainable and undisrupted. The latter is suitable only for the scrutinizing human, and the ways are disrupted. It is so because since its repayment is delayed, he becomes suitable for disruptions and preventions that confuse him in his work.

The Power of Payment Is the Power of Reward

Conscious repayment, sensual repayment: These are human repayment and beastly repayment, which are the two forces of Providence, by which animals do the tasks they are assigned by His Providence.

The Standard for the Sages

Indeed, there are many degrees in the human species itself, for it is measured by the sense of development of each one, and by the measure of one's retreat from the beastly world and into the human world. When one is insufficiently developed, one cannot wait for the payment very long, and chooses works with instantaneous reward, even if for a lower price. A more developed person might wait and choose works that pay better, even if the payment comes after a very long time. Know that this is the standard for the sages, for it depends on the material development of each one, and anyone who can prolong the repayment can get a bigger reward.

What Is Development?

Therefore, you will see that the majority of the learned ones, as soon as they have completed their learning and can enjoy the fruits of their work, they abandon the study and go out to trade with the people and be rewarded. But the minority, restrain themselves and continue to learn, each according to one's own talents. It is so because they want to receive a greater reward, such as to be among the greatest in the generation or innovators. Naturally, after some time their peers become very jealous of them.

The Power of the Goal

Know that this is the standard for development of the generations, meaning the power to restrain and prolong the time of repayment, and choose the higher sum. For this reason, in those generations great innovators proliferated because in our generations there are more with this kind of talent. Their exertion is immeasurable because their sense of restraining is highly developed, both for prolonging the time, and for exerting.

Returning Power or "Causal Power"

There is no movement among all the animals that is not repaid. It is called the "Power of the Goal," and the degrees are evaluated only according to the sensation of the reward, meaning by development. The more one is developed, the more one senses. Hence, the power of the goal acts in such a person to a greater extent, and can significantly increase and enhance one's effort.

The second one is the above-stated, meaning the "power of anticipation for the time of repayment." That causal power is evaluated by two: the first is the sense of the price. That sensation is the sum of the price, where one who is more sensitive is also more expensive and the causal power is increased.

The second is the power to wait for a later time, for even a higher price requires having a more developed body, which can sense the remoteness. Also, any development that unfolds in the human species is only those two above-mentioned sensations: the sensation of price, and the sensation of remoteness, and the measure of wisdom rises through them to its apex.

Practical Kabbalah

Know that the governance of the above-mentioned sensations are sensed primarily in those who attain, since the pleasantness of each degree is so great, and its reward is always near, so one has no reason to be in pain and climb to a higher degree.

The Spirit of Pleasure and Intellectual Pleasure

Moreover, there are spirit and wisdom here, and they are one. But in regard to the receiver, who consists of body and mind, they are sensed as two forces: the body has a calm spirit, and the mind has great intellect. For this reason, the body must lose of its spirit when it rises to receive knowledge and reason.

3. THE ESSENCE OF MYSTERY AND ITS DEPARTMENTS

Below, I wish to give the reader a clear understanding of the prohibition to use practical Kabbalah, as well as witchcraft and forms of prevalent esotericism, in order to provide a sound basis from which to extend scientific research.

In our time, many scholars have delved over this issue, exerting to lay a scientific, empiric basis under this matter. Indeed, they have given it much thought. To the best of my knowledge, they have not found any scientific basis that is worth consideration due to their lack of knowledge concerning the origin of this esotericism, which the human mind cannot reach.

What has brought me to touch upon that topic is that I saw the ignorance of the masses as far as discerning such matters, causing them to mix together various forms of esotericism. For this reason I have now come to show the origin and foundation of this type of esotericism.

I have already explained in part one [here] that there are three parts in the wisdom of the hidden, being material, figurative, and practical learning. In the third part, called "practical learning," I explained how practical Kabbalists work not according to nature, since they have retreated to the initial degrees where there are plentiful pleasantness and sweetness. For this reason, their vital spirit significantly increases, such as you see among ordinary people, whose strong will power activates the ones whose desire is weaker, forcing them to act as they wish, and without any thinking or understanding, or any benefit for themselves, they follow and obey their every wish.

Similarly, when one who has attained exerts to attain those degrees that yield great vitality and spirit, they can activate it in their friends to a certain extent, as well. It is so because the nature of the spiritual is as the nature of the fish at sea, where the big swallows the small when it thinks of it. And here, only thought acts, and the rest is indeed not thought but desire and spirit, since a thought does not move even the thinker himself, so how will it move another? Instead, the desire receives and is depicted according to the image of that thought of the one with the bigger desire, and acts in the smaller one. Psychologists define it as "power of thought," but it is a mistake because it is a desire and not a thought.

Also, know that this active power is so mighty that it can induce imaginations in one's friend to the exact same extent that every person has the power to imagine in one's own mind. And as far as dominion, it is much more powerful than the one who imagines in one's own mind. It is so because one who depicts by himself has the power of intellectual critique opposite the imagination. If it denies that imagination, that imagination is weakened and cannot work at all.

This is not so when one is activated by another. At that time, one is in a state of anarchy, without any work of one's machine, called "the brain." For this reason, there will never be any criticism, but the imagination he has obtained from the other works in him as though he had long ago agreed to it wholeheartedly, and above any criticism, as though it is a type of prejudice.

Moreover, one can clothe and suck the spirit of one's friend inside until he feels his feelings—to an extent—and even his memories, and can contemplate them and determine which of them is desirable and notify him. This is why it is written that they "deny the household of above," for although only the foul ones have come to them, they remain and use them permanently, and intensify their vital spirit more than genuine sages.

Three Thirds in the Concealment of the Wisdom

There are three thirds in the concealment of the wisdom of truth. The first is the unnecessary; the second is the impossible; and the third is "The glory of God is in the concealment of a matter." I will clarify them one at a time.

The First Third: Unnecessary

This part has no loss in it at all, of course, except for the matter of cleanness of the mind, since we find that triviality is the most harmful saboteur. All the destructors the world are "triviality" people, meaning contemplate trivial matters and announce trivial announcements. This is why we do not accept a disciple before he has sworn to remove himself from these saboteurs.

Second Third: Impossible

This part, of course, requires no oath. However, because it is possible to disclose it by mistaken words, and to take pride in it in the eyes of the masses, it is included in the oath, as well.

Third Third: The Glory of God
Is in the Concealment of a Matter

This part is the gravest in the concealment, for it has caused many casualties. Know that all the sorcerers that ever were, and all the cunning ones, come only from such disclosures, where immature disciples erred in the matters and went out to teach anyone they came across, without considering if they were fit for it. They went out and used the wisdom for human purposes—for lust and honor—and they have taken the sanctities of the Lord to secularism and to the street. This is what is called "practical Kabbalah."

The Meaning of Conception and Birth

1) RULES

General and Particular

The scrutiny of the educated in creation, in the first concept, is defined as emulating the work of the Creator. The work of the Creator is called "Providence," or the "nature of creation."

They are not called "body," but rather "simple matter of flesh and blood in its still (inanimate) form," completely amorphous. It is so because anything that is called by the name, "form," is regarded as a spiritual force and is not a body.

This gives us a law by which all bodies are equal. However, as Earth is a single body that cannot be divided into many—for we do not find any change of form in it from one part to another—the still cannot be divided into many elements.

Also, all the power of multiplication in the world is a wonderful, spiritual force. For this reason, anything that is general is suitable and praiseworthy, for it comes from the spiritual force, and anything that is particular is contemptible and lowly. This designates the difference between a selfish person and one who is dedicated to one's nation.

There is no doubt that the merit of the collective is defined by its power of multiplicity, for if we have decided that the power of multiplicity is a spiritual and important matter, then if the multiplicity is greater, he is more important.

It follows that one who is dedicated to one's nation is more important than one who is dedicated to one's town, and one who is dedicated to the world is more important than one who is dedicated to one's nation. This is the first concept.

Birth in Spirituality

Therefore, as there is birth for an individual, in relation to the construction of the bodies, there is birth for the collective. This is done by renewal of the spiritual force, meaning development of the concepts is birth for the collective, for in the spiritual, disparity of form divides the worlds from one another. This birth means arriving at the world of correction.

The Exodus from Egypt Is Called Birth

If we are speaking of the multiplication in the spiritual essence, it is similar to the corporeal case of being born from the mother's womb—which is a dark and spoiled world, with all kinds of filth and unpleasantness—into a world lit up by perfection, the world of correction.

By that we understand the meaning of the preparation as defined in the kingdom of the priests, who have come to it by the prophecy of Moses, and for which they were rewarded with freedom from the angel of death and the reception of the Torah.

At that time they needed a new birth into the air of the enlightened world, called in the verse, "A pleasant land, good and broad."

Born Dead

That newborn was born dead because after the pregnancy—which is the iron melting pot and the enslavement in Egypt—came the birth. But they were still unfit to breathe the spirit of life from the enlightened world, where they were guaranteed to come, until the count began, and the war with Amalek, and the trials with the water, etc., and they arrived at the Sinai desert. Sinai (as our sages said) means *Sinaa* (hatred), for they are pronounced the same, meaning the affliction entailed in every illness.

The Birth to Father and Mother

At that time they became worthy of breathing the spirit of life, and the prophecy, "And you shall be unto Me a kingdom of priests and a holy nation," came true in them. First, the kingdom of priests, to revoke their personal possessions, and subsequently the holy nation, which is to bestow contentment upon their Maker through "love your neighbor as yourself."

In corporeality, the newborn falls into loving and loyal hands, who are the father and the mother, who guarantee its sustenance and health. Likewise, once each one has been prepared with 600,000 who care for one's sustenance, they breathe the spirit of life, as it is written, "And Israel encamped there before the mount," and RASHI interpreted, "as one man with one heart."

2) POSTERIOR AND ANTERIOR

Man's eyes are before him. This implies that he can look only to the future, in a manner of growth from below upward. However, he cannot look behind him, in the manner of conception, from above downward (as it is written about Lot, "Look not behind you").

For this reason, man is denied any real knowledge because he is devoid of the beginning. He is like a book whose first half is missing, so its content cannot be understood at all. The whole advantage of those who attain is that they are rewarded with attaining the conception, too, meaning the progression from above downward.

Man includes everything, and it is evidently seen when he looks and contemplates something. Everyone knows that he is not looking outside his own body and ideas whatsoever, yet he attains the whole world, knows what people think, assesses how to be liked by them, and adapts himself to their wishes.

In order to know that, he only needs to look inside himself, and he already understands his contemporaries. It is so because everyone is equal, and a person contains all the people within. The restriction on one's knowledge is that one does not know one's own conception nor remembers anything from that time so as to be able to say anything about it.

The Fiftieth Gate

This is the meaning of the verse, "and you will see My back, but My face shall not be seen." Moses attained the meaning of conception, meaning all the discernments from above downward, in full. It is called "the posterior of the spiritual worlds," and all he lacked was to look at the "face," as well, meaning to see the future through the end of the correction. This is called "fifty gates of *Bina*," since the level of *Bina* is one hundred gates, and *Bina* is named by Kabbalists, *Ima* (mother), as she is the mother of the whole world. One who is rewarded with attaining all one hundred gates in her is rewarded with the revelation of completeness.

Their fifty gates from behind are the conception, meaning the progression from above downward, and their fifty gates from before are the necessary path of development through the end of correction. At that time, "The whole earth shall be full of the knowledge of the Lord," and "They shall teach no more each man his neighbor and each man his brother saying 'Know the Lord,' for they shall all know Me, from the least of them to the greatest of them."

This is the meaning of Moses' prayer, "Show me please Your glory," meaning all fifty gates of *Bina* from within. And the Creator said to him, "You shall see My back"; it is enough that you see all fifty in My posterior, from above downward. "But My face shall not be seen," since you will not see all the fifty from before, "For man shall not see Me and live," meaning before it is due time, when the vessels have fully adapted and developed.

Prior to that, one must die by seeing this because the vessels will not be able to receive that great light and will be cancelled. This is the meaning of what is written, "Fifty gates of *Bina* (intelligence) were created in the world, and all but one were given to Moses."

But in spirituality there is no lack. Rather, it is all or nothing, as in "A slightly broken vow is a completely broken vow." But in the end, when the measure of the vessels grow and develop sufficiently, they will be fit for attaining the fiftieth gate. (You should also know that there are two kinds of attainment: prophecy and wisdom. With respect to wisdom, Moses attained what all the sages attained. But with respect to prophecy, he could not attain. It is about that that our sages said, "A sage is preferable to a prophet," and they also said that Solomon attained the fiftieth gate.)

The Soul Begets the Body: Conception and Growth

We find two progressions in a sown wheat:

1. From the time it is placed in the ground, when it begins to strip itself of its form. This is regarded as

begetting, until it becomes naught, meaning the substrate of negation of its progenitors' form, and the actual becomes potential. Until then it is regarded as conception, extending from the progression from above downward.

2. When it comes to the final point, the growth begins. This is the progression from below upward, until it obtains the level of its progenitor.

General and Particular Are the Same

General and particular are as identical as two drops in a pond. It is so both externally, in the state of the planet in general, and internally, for even in the smallest atom we find a complete system of sun and planets circling it, just as in the universe. Likewise, man is the internality of the world, and you find within man all the images of the upper worlds, *Atzilut*, *Beria*, *Yetzira*, and *Assiya*. It is as Kabbalists said, "*Atzilut* is the *Rosh* (head), *Beria* is up to the *Chazeh* (chest), *Yetzira* is from there to *Tabur* (navel), and *Assiya* is from the *Tabur* down."

For this reason, there is a progression from above downward in man's conception, too, meaning a slow expansion from the progenitor, the mother, until one completely detaches from her as one emerges to the world, moving from operating to operated, from the authority of the progenitor to one's own authority.

At that time begins the progression from below upward, the days of nursing, when still attached to the mother's breasts, until the form is fully completed in the final level of the progenitors.

However, *Adam HaRishon* (the first man) was a creation of the Creator. He was certainly not born from a woman, but from the dust of the earth, as were the rest of the first creations, who were formed from that dust, as it is written, "All was from the dust." And yet, that dust extends from the upper worlds that precede it.

It is so because above, too, there are light and vessel. The light is in the forms in the reception, and the vessel is the will to receive those suitable forms. That vessel, which is the will to receive, is never constant, neither in terms of importance, nor in terms of an independent reality that stands in and of itself, but only with what it receives. For this reason, it has no more merit than what is being received.

For example, a poor man who wishes to acquire wealth is no more important than a poor man who is content with his lot and does not aspire for wealth. On the contrary, he is worse than him because the will to receive becomes one with the received matter, and they are only two halves of one thing. When each half is separated, it has no value in itself, which you can discuss with or negotiate.

3) What Is a Soul?

The Law of Development according to the Wisdom of Kabbalah

It is impossible to examine anything before you see it from its beginning to its end. And since one feels only what comes from within (just as physicians have found that the colors are not the same in both eyes, but there is rather an agreement here), therefore, first one must know oneself through and through, at least since the time of conception (impregnation) to the time of adulthood. And because this is not so, for one begins to know oneself only when becoming a complete human being, one is therefore devoid of the ability to self-scrutinize.

No Person Knows Himself

The second reason is that to know something you must primarily observe its negative qualities. And one cannot see one's own faults (and to the same extent that one can borrow from what one sees in others, one looks in a mirror that does not illuminate). It is so because anything bad that one must receive comes to one as pleasure, for otherwise he would not receive it. Also, it is a law that wherever there is pleasure, a person does not regard it as bad, except after many experiences that develop in them. However, this requires days and years, as well as memory, conclusions, and observations, of which not everyone is capable. For this reason, no person knows himself.

But Kabbalists have attainment, and attain a matter in full. That is, they are rewarded with attaining all those degrees in reality that one can attain. This is considered that they have attained a matter in full, and that complete matter is called a "soul."

That Soul Is the Possession of *Adam HaRishon*

I have already explained above, in item 2, that the worlds are attained in two ways—from above downward and from below upward. First, one attains from above downward, the hanging down of the soul. Subsequently comes from below upward, being the attainment itself.

The first progression is called *Ibur* (impregnation) because it is tantamount to a drop that gradually detaches from the father's brain, and is impregnated in the mother until it emerges to the world. This is regarded as the last degree from above downward, meaning taking into consideration the cause of the newborn. After all, until then it was still connected in some part to its mother and father, meaning the cause, and as it came into the world it became independent, and this is the order from above downward.

And the reason for all that is that His thought is unique. Hence, all incidents are the same, and the general is similar to the particular.

Conception and Growth of a Body as a Soul

From the moment of one's birth, when at the farthest point, begins the return to attainment, from below upward. This is called the "Law of Development," and it follows the exact same ways and inlets that descended from above downward.

Kabbalists attain it, but to corporeal eyes they seem as ordinary states—slow, gradual—until one's level grows to become like one's father and mother. At that time one is regarded as having attained all the degrees from below upward, meaning a complete degree.

4) FROM ABOVE DOWNWARD AND FROM BELOW UPWARD

The Growth Testifies to the Conception

And since the two progressions, from above downward and from below upward, are as similar as two drops in a pond, we can understand the progression from above downward by observing the progression from below upward, which is the second progression of the development, namely the growth.

Thus, you find that there are four states in the four worlds, ABYA, beginning with *Assiya*, such as when examining the progression of the growth of a fruit from the planting to its complete ripening.

1. Before the signs of ripening appear in it, which are all the laws of the states in the fruit. This is the world of *Assiya*.

2.   From the time when you can eat it and be satiated, although it is still tasteless. This is *Yetzira*.

3.   From the time when some flavor can be detected in it. This is *Beria*.

4.   From the time when its full flavor and beauty appear, and it is *Atzilut*. This order is from below upward.

Every Emanated and Born Comes in Two Ways

The whole issue of from above downward and from below upward that was explained in the four worlds, *ABYA*, applies even to the smallest item in the worlds, meaning in every cause and consequence. A cause is the father, the root, the agent. A consequence means that it was operated and done by the cause. For this reason, it is regarded as an offspring, a branch, or an extension and cause.

The meaning of these two progressions is understood in the particular just as in the general. From above downward is a way of separating the cause from its consequence until it emerges and becomes an authority on its own. And from below upward is the law of development that awakens it to grow from below upward until it attains its cause. That is, it becomes completely equal to it.

As we have explained above, the corporeal father and offspring that comes from the father's brain to the birth is the time of the ascent from below upward. You should discern likewise in all four types: still, vegetative, animate, and speaking.

As it is in the emanation of the elements of spirituality, so it is in all the worlds. It is so because from one [*Ehad* (unique)] emerges the *Yechida* (also unique), and all the ways that that *Yechida* received necessitate all the subsequent successions, both in the general and in the particular.

5) Emulating Creation

Birth of the Happy Humanity

When looking at the seal of the work of creation, we find there the words, "Which God has created to do." This means that the work of the Creator, which is set in the creation before us, is given to us in order to do and to add to it. Otherwise, the words "to do" would have been completely redundant and meaningless, and it would have to say, "For in it He rested from all His work which God has created." So why were the words, "to do," added here? It must be that this verse teaches us that the full extent of the work that the Creator has left in creation is in the exact measure, no more and no less, but the extent that enables us to perform its development and completion by ourselves.

In truth, our entire development in creation is but emulation of it. All the flavors and beauty of colors that we innovate and devise are but emulation of the tasteful colors that we find in colors. And likewise, from where does the carpenter know about making a four legged table, if not by emulating the work of the Creator, who has made creations that stand on four legs? Or, from where would he know about combining two pieces of wood if not by emulating the organs of the body, which are joined together, so he went and built in the wood accordingly?

People observe and study the reality set before us in perfect reason and beauty. Afterward, when they understand it, they emulate and do likewise. Subsequently, that example becomes a basis for another example, until man has created a handsome world full of inventions.

By looking at creation, planes were built with wings similar to birds. A radio was built to receive sound waves like the ears. In short, all of our successes are presented before us in creation and in reality as is, and all we need is to emulate it, and do.

Reality and the Existence of Reality Deny One Another

Reality—meaning reality in general, and all its parts that are created as creations in relation to that which belongs to their existence—we find that it is well set up, with every beauty and pleasantness, without any deficiency whatsoever. Truly, an enlightened world. But when we place opposite that the existence of this reality, meaning the manners by which these creations feed and sustain themselves, they are awry, disordered, tasteless, and very unrestrained. However, we have already explained about reality and the existence of reality in general in the essay, "The Meaning of Unity," and learn it from there.

Conclusion and Birth

From all this you should know that the general is always equal to the particular, that the Creator in and of Himself does not feel the multiplicity, as He is always in the singular authority, and you can conclude the benefit of the collective from that of the individual.

And as the existence and birth of the individual—which the Creator has set up naturally—is tested from the moment of birth and emergence to the place that the Creator has prepared, which is called "this world," it is considered that He has made certain that one will fall into the hands of loyal lovers who will tend, heal, and care for all of one's needs in complete devotion and love.

The same is true of the collective. If it wishes to be born and emerge to the world corrected for the whole collective, it is necessary to see that this general child falls into the hands of loyal parents who will love it just as devotedly as would a father and a mother, meaning through the commandment of love of others. This is similar to the preparation for the giving of Torah.

However, here we will engage only in the human species, and see how much of the pleasantness and good the work of the Creator has sets up concerning one's existence, to keep one until one is worthy of being called upon, in the shape of a working human. And when we take the order of one's own existence, how much of the loathed and terrible is in it—wherever one turns, one condemns, and one's very existence is built on the ruin of one's neighbor.

6) THE CORRECTED AND THE NEEDY OF MAN'S WORK

Which God Has Created to Do

Know that the Creator needed the work of creation only to the extent that human power could not work there. Similar to digestion, the Creator created everything in such a way that the digestion of the food in our stomach happens without effort on our part.

However, from the point where one can work—as this is all the flavor and contentment of the Creator, who wanted to enjoy His work, meaning to fashion creations that can add, delight, and please like Him, but has no wish whatsoever to cook our food, which is on the stove for us without our awareness, since we can do it by ourselves.

This is similar to a teacher and a student, where the whole intention of the teacher is to give the student the strength to be like him, and to teach other students, like him. Also, the Creator is pleased when His creations create and innovate like Him. Yet, our whole power to innovate and develop is not real innovation. Rather, it is a type of emulation. And the more the emulation matches the work of nature, to that extent is our level of development measured.

From this we know that we have the power to correct ourselves, the existence of reality, like nature's pleasant example of reality. The proof of that is that if the Creator had not worked His full Providence in that discernment, too, for "Is the Lord's hand short?" but it is rather necessary that in this place, which is our own correction, we are able to correct ourselves.

7) MOVEMENT AS A SIGN OF LIFE

Still, Vegetative, Animate—Speaking

With regard to spiritual life, people are divided into two: 1) still, vegetative, animate; 2) speaking. The still, vegetative, and animate are regarded as completely lifeless. The speaking is regarded as living.

Life is the power of movement. It is known that the beginning of life is done by two completely opposite actions.

When the speaking is born, it is also regarded as lifeless, until it is awakened through pushes, since its vessels are ready to receive life and movement while still in the mother's womb. Upon the emergence to the world, the air of the world affects it with chilliness to which it is not accustomed, which causes the awakening of the contraction.

And after the first contraction it must spread once more to its former measure. These two things—contraction and expansion—are the first step that gives it life.

However, sometimes, due to weakness of the birth, the fetus weakens and the contraction is not awakened in it, since the reception of the chilliness of the air of the world is too weak to affect its contraction. This causes it to be born dead, meaning that it still did not have a place and a reason for life—which begin with contraction—to clothe in it.

Without internal contraction there is no expansion. It is so because it by no means expands more than its boundary, so there is no movement. And the sign of a creature that is ready for the light of life is that it at least has the power to contract for some reason. At that time comes the light of life and makes the expansion, and the first movement of life occurs. For this reason, movement will not cease from it and becomes a living, moving being.

That first movement is called "a soul," meaning the spirit of life that breathes in his nostrils, as it is written, "and breathed into his nostrils the breath of life."

However, the still, vegetative, and animate do not possess that power to make an internal contraction, for whatever reason. And because this is so, it is impossible for the light of life to clothe in them and cause expansion.

He has given an inexorable law that without contraction and expansion, the vessel will not be able to expand beyond its boundary. For this reason, the still, vegetative, and animate are destined to be forever lifeless.

But the speaking is truly fit for life. However, it is born dead, as was said above, since it requires some reason and cause that will act upon it and at least make the first contraction. This happens to it by the cold air that comes to it from Torah and good deeds.

The Quality of the Contraction

The contraction should be by the power of the creature itself. We discern two kinds of contraction: 1) contraction as a result of an external cause, such as coolness; 2) contraction that comes from the vessel itself.

1.   As you see when spanking and pressing the newborn to wake it up, although each press and spank causes a contraction in the newborn's body, the expansion

returns. It does not return because of the light of life, but because of the structure of the vessel itself, which must always maintain its exact boundary and custom. For this reason, when some element comes and presses it, the vessel has the power to return to its place, by the force that causes its positive boundary.

2. But if the contraction happens from within the vessel itself, and not due to an external cause, then it cannot return to its previous boundary whatsoever because the contraction that took place in it was from its own structure. Thus, it is impossible for it to return to its original boundary.

The Creator is the exception, meaning that a new, personal light should expand in it, return it to its custom, where that light is added to the original light, to be in it permanently. That is, each time it contracts, the light returns and causes it to expand to its previous size. That light is called "life."

Two Contractions—Partial and General. Opposite Them, Two Expansions

The blood is the soul. It is so because the red color needs the white color to connect to it, and then it is called "blood." Before it has permanently joined it, it is not regarded as blood because at that time there are lying and rising in it. This is so because its nature is O-Dem (two Hebrew words that mean "or blood" or "or stillness"), and then irregular rising is painted in it, which is only called "the color O-Dem," from the words, "Be still for the Lord." For this reason, the colors fall from it again and it becomes white, colorless, which is irregular lying (resting).

And when the two join, they become tendons of life's blood.

When the two become tendons of life's blood, making the contradictions in it, one becomes the living soul, meaning the O is cut off from the *Odem* (red), leaving *Dam* (blood) permanently. And yet, the lying and rising that were before conjoin even now, in this blood.

Hence, we discern two kinds in blood: red and white. That is, the same red and white that were operating one at a time before, have now conjoined and made that blood, which is called a "living soul." Know that this is the meaning of the partial contraction and partial expansion, which are called *Nefesh* (soul) and *Ruach* (spirit).

However, that light, which made the expansion—the partial of the soul—is a general, wonderful upper light. For this reason, it fills and complements every kind of contraction inscribed in that structure.

It is known that there was already white in that body, in the part that is unfit to receive the *O-Dem* color (red), since ... of the red were robbed and fell when they join together in vain, etc. For this reason, once the light has completed the first expansion of the light of the above-mentioned living soul, it refills that old contraction that was made in it initially. This is what is called "general expansion," or "tendons of the brain," extending from the red material, whose form has been completely wiped away.

This is the meaning of what is written, "And breathed into his nostrils" (in Hebrew it is written, "noses"), two noses. The first nose is of red-white. The second nose is of the white that is completely wiped away. "And the man became a living soul," first out of the red-white nose, which is the blood and the first expansion, but finally it was the soul of life because it expanded in the second nose, as well, the wiped away white, which is a soul and regarded as GAR.

You should also know that the first expansion of tendons of blood relates to the bottom, bodily brain, called marrow, which is there. ...operating without one's awareness since the intermediate state, from the first nose to the second nose, is the time of nurturing of ... ... and then the light works completely without one's awareness, for he has not attained his soul.

And the second expansion in the tendons from marrows kept for it as the second oppositeness, which is called the "second nose," is the relation of the upper brain: ... ... to the three *Mochin* that operate consciously in him. This is called ...

Oppositeness between Head and Body

It has been explained that in the tendons from the marrow, the red is on the right. This is the color and the being that is formed on this paper. The white is the complete left, for the second nose is also erased from it, and even the color disappears from it, so that the red is the being and the white is the absence.

The opposite of it is blood tendons, since the red is the left, meaning O that has been joined in advance, and as "river and maybe." Conversely, although the white is lying, this image still becomes right and rising. For this reason, it is an eternal soul, which does no longer needs color. And the red color that remains and is inscribed in advance has now been put to the left, in *Gevura*. It is called *Dam* (blood) without the O (of *Odem* [red]), so that the white is on the right, for it is not needed, and the red color will not occur in it, and the red is regarded as left, only *Gevura*, which is called "blood."

Here you need to understand that the *Reshimo* (recollection) of the above-mentioned red in the first nose—and their tendons, which rose to the left, after the second nose, regarded as soul—is erased and permanently passes away from this structure. For this reason, the head, the brain, is white without any red at all.

Ibur (Conception)

During pregnancy, the fetus is merely a vegetative. Its movements are not regarded as movements of life, since the movements are done by its mother, of which the fetus is part.

Its environment is called "abdomen," and the mother is the boundary of the environment that is cast upon it, and it eats what its mother eats, etc. And the birth begins with the head.

The Essence of Life

Knowing the living is the self-essence. Movement is defined by contraction (see above) for no creation can extend its boundary even as a hairsbreadth.

This extends from the head, for there the giving of this power is restricted to slightly less than its boundary, regarding the question.

You should know that as long as another force contracts it below its size, this does not make the inanimate animate. Rather, it must contract of its own. But how can this be while it is still inanimate? This requires a prayer to be rewarded with the upper force.

By that we can understand the concealed under the surrounding light, and the meaning of "for man shall not see Me and live," for the living can move, and if it still cannot contract then it is not alive, but still. This is the meaning of "The righteous' death is with a kiss," meaning they lose the power of contraction.

From My Flesh I Shall See God

QUALIFICATION FOR THE NURTURING OF THE SOUL

It is impossible to sustain one's body in the world without a certain amount of knowledge about the corporeal nature, such as knowing which drugs are lethal, and what things burn and do harm, as well as knowledge and assessment of what is in one's friend's heart, without which it is impossible to exist in the material world.

Just so, man's soul cannot exist in the next world until it has acquired a certain amount of the nature of the systems of the spiritual worlds, their changes, couplings, and generations.

We discern three periods in the body: The first is from the time of birth, when one has no knowledge whatsoever, and all that is required to know in order to exist comes from the father and mother, and one is sustained by their keeping and wisdom. This state is the first *Katnut* (nursing).

The second is when a person has grown and acquired some knowledge. At that time one can keep from things that harm one's body through joint keeping—that of the father and mother, and that of one's own. This is the second *Katnut*.

The third is the state of *Gadlut* (adulthood), when one has acquired sufficient knowledge for life, to look after oneself enough to survive. At that time one departs the authority of one's father and mother and acquires self-rule. This is the third state, the state of *Gadlut*.

Likewise, concerning the soul, a person reincarnates until one acquires the wisdom of truth in full. Without them, the soul cannot reach its full level. But it is not that the knowledge one has acquired raises the level of the soul. Rather, it is the soul's inherent nature that it will not grow by its own effort before it has acquired the knowledge of the spiritual nature. Its growth depends on the measure of its knowledge.

The reason this is so is that if it could grow without knowing, it would be harmed, like an infant who is ignorant and cannot walk. If it could walk on its own feet, it would throw itself into a fire.

However, the growth comes primarily through good deeds, which depend on attaining the wisdom of truth. And both—the knowledge and the good deeds—depend on attaining the wisdom of truth. And for the above reason, both come together. This is the meaning of, "If you know not ... go forth," "go forth and see," etc.

Therefore, each complete soul attains all the souls from *Adam HaRishon* to the end of correction, as one perceives one's acquaintances and neighbors, and according to one's knowledge guards oneself from them, or connects and lives with them. And it is not surprising that one attains all the souls, since spirituality does not depend on time or place, and there is no death there.

BODY AND SOUL

Every body is impatient and ill-tempered, for its livelihood is through incarnations through the seven years of famine and the seven years of abundance. It is an inexorable law that the years of famine cause the years of abundance to be forgotten and the body reincarnates between them like stones grinded by water. And another plight awaits all around it—it imagines that one's friend is happy and content.

This comes because at its basis, the soul is grinded between the good inclination and the evil inclination. It incarnates between them, at times feeling relief by the surrounding good inclination, and at times suffering an additional plight by the surrounding evil inclination.

OBTAINING KNOWLEDGE IN CORPOREALITY AND IN SPIRITUALITY

The connection between the body and the soul is only that in the former, things happen to it naturally and by themselves, and in the latter they happen through work and joint relation between the spiritual and the corporeal.

The advantage of the spiritual over the corporeal is that in the corporeal there is reality even without attaining all the incidents, similar to the perception of an infant, who does not know the reason for the thing, and will also not eat something that is harmful. But in the spiritual, no reality is attained prior to knowing the events and their outcomes. To the extent of the knowledge of the events, so is the attainment of one's own greatness, and the attainment of the surrounding spiritual reality.

REVELATION OF THE WORKS OF THE CREATOR—IN CONCEALMENT

"Then I was by Him as a master craftsman; and I was daily a delight." Our sages interpreted it to mean, to inform, that prior to the days of the Messiah, when receiving proselytes, the craftsmen come out toward them, and each craftsman plays with him. On the first day he reveals the light, on the second he makes the firmament, etc. These are the six workdays, and all delight in resting on the seventh day, placing in it sanctity and blessing to the worlds.

This is the meaning of what our sages said, that prior to bringing the first fruit, all the craftsmen stand before them. That is, precisely when they are called "wise." However, the craftsmen do not stand before disciples of the wise. Come and see how great is a commandment in its time.

The merit of the Sabbath is that in it is the blessing and sanctity to correct all the weekdays. And although it seems as though the correction depends on the work days and not on the days of rest, in which one does not work at all, it is not so. Rather, the blessing and sanctity of the Sabbath corrects the weekdays.

Indeed, each correction seemingly requires work. But in truth, the power of the Creator appears in full only in concealment, for when the power of concealment disappears from the world, perfection promptly appears by itself. And as one who throws one's staff to the firmament, the staff flies up because the power of the thrower is in it. Therefore, the entire duration of the flight is attributed to the power of the thrower. Also, the strength of the thrower appears at that time.

Conversely, during its whole return and fall toward the earth, the power of the thrower is not attributed to the fall at all. Rather, it returns to its root by itself, without any assistance.

Similarly, in all the concealments, the work of the Creator is apparent. But in the return to perfection, no work or power are required because in the absence of the preventing force, it returns to its root and perfection by itself.

This is the meaning of, "And God rested on the seventh day ... for in it, He rested from all His work." That is, on that day the power of the work of the Creator was removed from the world, after having worked to establish it in its current form throughout the work days. But on the seventh day, no power worked, but it was left alone, as it is written, "And I will take away My hand." Thus, naturally, the force of perfection is imprinted specifically on that day so that the power of concealment will not work here.

Attaining the Spiritual Form

It is likewise in attaining the spiritual form. The attaining errs in its two forms: 1) that it will not be imaginary whatsoever; 2) that its attainment will be beyond any doubt, just as one does not doubt one's own existence.

The title, "spiritual," indicates that it is resembled to the wind (in Hebrew *Ruach* means both "spirit" and "wind"), where although the wind has no edge, similitude, or appearance, no person doubts its existence, since one's life depends on it. If the wind is sucked out of a house, should an animal be taken there, it will die. Hence, its existence is obvious for it is one's life.

And from the corporeal we can understand the spiritual: The essence of the inner mind is similar to the interior of the body, which is called "the soul of every flesh," regarded as *HaVaYaH* with its deficiency.

Likewise, the internality of the mind, called "the intellectual soul," is also deficient *HaVaYaH*.

It is so because such a being, which feels its existence, feels its deficiencies. This is not so in animals, which are completely devoid of that perception and are completely devoid of the intellectual soul and its internality.

Because of it, they feel its deficiency to the extent required for their physical existence. Its vitality is measured by the extent of the consistency of the sensation of lack. And if it does not feel a lack, it cannot feed itself and continue its existence, and it dies. Moreover, its size and health depend on the sensation of the lack, like the corporeal body, where the healthier also has a greater appetite, and therefore eats more, and thus grows bigger and healthier.

THE NEED TO ATTAIN THE EMANATOR

We must still know the lack that the intellectual soul feels. Let me tell you that it is the need to attain its emanator, for it is engraved in its nature to crave to know its emanator and creator, since it feels its own existence. That is, it has been prepared *by default* to search what is above.

It cannot be said that this lack is not defined in attaining its emanator, but that it rather pursues all the secrets and wishes to know about supernatural things and incarnations, and about what is in one's friend's heart, and so forth.

This is not according to the rule that I have written above, that the internality of the matter is that which does not extend oneself. If it were, a lack for attainment would be depicted only in its maker. But it is clear that only this attainment is an internal lack, which is not called "an offshoot." But an inquiry in the creatures is an extension toward others, for had there not been creations in the world—such as if it were the only creation—it would not have been pursuing to attain them whatsoever.

But attaining its emanator is a deficiency toward itself, and this is its being. That is, it feels itself as an emanated being. All its events aim toward it, and this is the deficiency that it feels— that it will be able to attain its emanator. And to the extent that it perceives that vision, we can accurately measure the size of its own body.

Attaining the Emanator

It is written, "For you did not see any image." This requires interpretation, for what fool would think and gather that there is any corporeal similitude in the Creator? But in truth, this is why there is attainment in the Creator in the world, for no desire awakens for that which does not exist in reality.

Rather, we can discuss this in the spiritual kind and in its ordinances, which is more spiritual than the whole of reality. This is the meaning of the mind, whose form grips man's sensation in discerning truth and falsehood. This distinction is called "the mind's body," according to the perception of the corporeal ones. For this reason, this discernment was defined as "part of God above," which is truly devoid of any similitude, but is only gripped in the senses and is called "a decision" or "reality," or "absence of reality," which is clarified in laws and ways. That verse is called "the body of the mind and its image." We can say about it that this verse is part of God above, for which this image is included in oneself and one's perception of oneself and one's existence.

The image in this verse is a complete and constant image of its situation, which cannot be completely annulled, or slightly. It is called "a proven and necessary form without additions or subtractions."

This is the meaning of "'I, and you shall not have,' we heard them from the Mighty One." The word, "I," also includes "You shall not have," meaning that if the Creator had necessarily been revealed to them, no law or warning would have been depicted— "You shall not have"—but the Creator would have been revealed to them by His will, and it would not be an imperative.

It is like a person who shows his wealth to his friend and tells him, "I can show it to you, but now you do not recognize my wealth at all. So exert yourself to remember this form, and then I will want to give you part of my wealth, let alone that you will see all my wealth, as long as you keep this form in your memory. That is, I did not give you that decision by an imperative on which there is no ruler. Rather, I am the ruler, for all the earth is mine." All the seeing is with His simple will. And when I want, you will not remember even what you saw in the vision. And when I do want, you will always see Me. Moreover, I will also remind you all the forgotten things. This is from the wonders of the Creator, who cannot be depicted by any intellect, meaning to grasp the matter in full while keeping that man's mind, and it is voluntary and not compulsory to remain for the governance of the upper one.

Recognizing the Attainment—Only by the Path of Torah

I wonder at the researchers of Godliness, whose entire research is a disgrace to us, for they exert to bring evidence to what is known and does not require evidence, and repel and slight what is concealed from the denial of the corporeal boundaries.

The truth is that the first perception does not need any philosophical proof, since it is the first concept wherever one turns. It is similar to asking a person, "Who wrote this wondrous book of wisdom?" And he answered that indeed, there is no such a sage in the world, but it just happened that his little boy spilled ink on those parchments, which then spread in the form of letters, creating these combinations in connections of wondrous words of wisdom.

Indeed, all concealments are from His Providence to the creatures, and their denial is also among the corporeal boundaries. But about this they keep utterly silent, for indeed it can only be kept in the way of Torah and Mitzvot (commandments), and not by any scrutiny in the world.

You should also know that the existence of realty must extend from the sensation of Providence. This is called "complete awareness," which brings with it His love and His pleasant bounty. It is not so with that which extends through the dry, intellectual scrutiny; this knowledge neither adds nor subtracts.

This is the meaning of what our sages said, that there is he who is present, and he who is absent. It follows that all the souls of Israel were present at the foot of Mount Sinai because from that event extend all the souls of Israel throughout the generations. It is as we said, that it concerns the bodily soul, which is *HaVaYaH* and its deficiency with it. Extending its vitality depends on determining the deficiency, for were the seeing not positive, the intellectual soul would not have been deficient any longer. Thus, it would not be able to eat to satiation, and would therefore be cancelled altogether.

But it is a wonder that the rule about seeing is that the desire promptly accompanies it without any forcing, and promptly gives nourishment to establish this desire, as it is written, "that your days may be multiplied," which is the keeping of the Torah and its statutes. In this way, the law about seeing is evident as though they have received it from Sinai today, and each day it is as new to them, for on that depends the law regarding seeing. But when they break any law in the Torah, they promptly remain in the dark, as blind people who have never seen light.

The Essence of the Intellectual Perception

You already know that the intellectual ones, with bodies, are not robbed of knowing their emanator whatsoever, just as they are not robbed of knowing their friends, who are like them. It is so because a friend, like a brother, does not recognize only their spirit and internality, without any clothing, since the mind itself is already wrapped in clothing, meaning the power of imagination.

And because one cannot imagine a spiritual form, that whole kind is invisible to him. And yet, his gaze constantly falls on the externality, meaning one's friend's body and physical movements. And by persistence, they will thoroughly recognize all the spiritual degrees in it, for this is all he wants to know, and not his own bodily flesh, of course.

He will not feel any lack or sadness at not knowing his mind and degrees in its actual spiritual form, for he is not obligated to know his friend more than he knows himself. And even his own internality he does not attain.

For this reason, when the creature is well versed in all the laws of nature and its corporeal ordinances, and observes them diligently, it can be said that he knows the Creator face to face. It is as one speaks to one's friend, where each of his parts is adhered to his friend in similarity, meaning a power of imagination of intellectual forms and movements.

And when we research the essence of the mind to the best of our ability, we will find that it is by the gathering of spiritual beings, and from that collection extends its "conducts." That is, all of man's advantage over the beast is that in man there is an organ that can gather within it spiritual beings.

Likewise, the advantage of one person over another is in the amount of the power of the above-mentioned extension, and in the forms of the beings themselves, for one extends important beings, and another—beings that are not so important.

The difference between a spiritual being and the governance is that a boundary of the being is an intellectual image that extends and is present in one's mind unchanged, meaning it cannot be explained through events that happen over time.

And the governance falls under the influence of time and place. It is just as one who is naturally stingy can give a big donation once in his life, due to the place or the timing.

EXTENSIONS THAT GATHER IN MAN'S MIND

Know that the above-mentioned preparation, called "man's mind," is like a drop from the extract of all the organs and qualities of the corporeal body. It becomes attached to the first extensions that gather and extend to one's mind.

For example, while still a child, a person watches the conducts of the world and its Creator. Some of them become attached to knowledge, some to wealth, and some to power. If he chooses the quality of knowledge, because he likes it, it follows that he drew into himself a good creation, from which good conducts will extend. But if he clings to wealth, it is said that he drew into his mind an inferior spiritual being.

Later, when he grows, he sees more measures. For example: One man leaves all his corporeal possessions and dedicates himself to learning, while another chooses learning, but still engages in worldly matters. If the child nurtures the merit of the first, then he has extended a good being into his mind. But if he favors the second one, then he has drawn into himself an inferior being.

Afterward come types of learning—from the Creator or from the creatures—and afterward he checks whether to receive reward or to not receive reward. All those images are created beings, and from that collection, one substance is made, titled "mind."

Inheritance of the Land

[From a manuscript]

Israel will not return to their land until they are all in one bundle.

Our sages said, "Israel will not be redeemed until they are all in one bundle."

2) We must understand how Israel's unity relates to redemption.

3) First we should consider the matter of "By what will I know," etc., "for your seed will be a stranger," etc., "and afterward they will come out with great substance." It is not clear how this is an answer to Abraham's question.

4) We should understand the whole matter of this creation, in which man suffers so, what is it for? Could He have not delighted His creations without all that?

5) It is written in the books that the souls cannot receive the good reward for which He has created the world and the souls if they do not have a vessel ready to receive. And the only way one can obtain that vessel is through labor and toil in observing the *Mitzvot* (commandments) through the pressure and the struggles that one fights with the evil inclination and the numerous

preventions and troubles. These affliction and labor in Torah and *Mitzvot* provide a vessel for the soul so it may be fit to receive all the delight and pleasure for which He has created all creations.

6) Now we can understand the words of Ben He He in the Mishnah, *Avot*, who said, "The reward matches the sorrow," meaning that the reward is measured by the amount of sorrow. This is perplexing, for how is one's sorrow related to one's reward?

7) With the above said, we can thoroughly understand that all the sorrow and labor that have been prepared in the world are to provide the vessel to receive with the good reward for labor in Torah and *Mitzvot*. Thus, naturally, the greater one's sorrow in Torah and *Mitzvot*, the greater is one's vessel for reception of a greater reward.

8) Now we can understand the Creator's answer to Abraham's question: "By what will I know," etc. Abraham's question was because he saw in the spirit of his holiness the great amount of good reward that Israel is destined to receive by inheriting the land, since observing the *Mitzvot* depends entirely on the land. This is why Abraham the patriarch wondered, "By what will I know that I will inherit it?" That is, "How will I know that the children of Israel will be rewarded with such great reward in such great abundance? From where would they have big vessels fit for such wondrous reception?"

In that regard, the Creator answered him: "Your seed will be a stranger and will serve them and will torment them four hundred years," etc., for then they will have great labor in Torah and *Mitzvot*. This is when he understood that in this way they will certainly obtain the great vessels of reception, and the reply was completely satisfactory.

9) It follows from our words that inheriting the land requires great preparation, since the virtue of Torah and *Mitzvot* depend entirely on that, as through it one is rewarded with all the abundance

and benefit that the Creator has contemplated with regard to all the souls of Israel before He had created them. This is also why Abraham the patriarch was perplexed and did not understand from where would they take such great vessels as to be rewarded with the holiness of the land. Finally, the Creator told him that laboring in Torah and *Mitzvot* in the Egyptian exile will provide them with these great vessels and they will be fit for the holy land.

10) This is perplexing: It is one thing with regard to those who engage in Torah, but what about those who engage in worldly matters, who are not at all prepared to engage in Torah? How will they be rewarded these vessels?

11) The answer is that this is why they said in the above-mentioned commentary that Israel are not redeemed before they are all in one bundle. It is so because all of Israel are actually one body, and each organ has its unique role. For example, the head contemplates intellect and reason; the hands work and provide nourishments for the head, while the head itself does not have to work. It does not need it because the hands are quite sufficient. Likewise, the hands do not need to contemplate how to work because the head is quite enough for this.

12) If Israel become one bundle, like a single body, where the workers—who are the hands—provide for the head, then the labor and sorrow of those who engage in Torah and work will compensate for the workers... and this clarifies the commentary [Israel are not redeemed until they are all] in one bundle, and "a redeemer has come to Zion."

600,000 Souls

It is said that there are 600,000 souls, and each soul divides into several sparks. We must understand how it is possible for the spiritual to divide, since initially, only one soul was created, the soul of *Adam HaRishon*.

In my opinion, there is indeed only one soul in the world, as it is written (Genesis, 2:7), "and breathed into his nostrils the breath of life."[6] The same soul exists in all the children of Israel, complete in each and every one, as in *Adam HaRishon*, since the spiritual is indivisible and cannot be cut—which is rather a trait of corporeal things.

Yet, saying that there are 600,000 souls and sparks of souls appears as though it is divided by the force of the body of each person. In other words, first, the body divides and completely denies him of the radiance of the soul, and by the force of the Torah and the *Mitzva*, the body is cleansed, and to the extent of its cleansing, the common soul shines upon him.

For this reason, two discernments were made in the corporeal body: In the first discernment, one feels one's soul as a unique organ, and does not understand that this is the whole of Israel. And this is truly a flaw; hence, it causes along with the above-mentioned.

---

6   Translator's note: In Hebrew, the words "soul" and "breath" are spelled the same.

In the second discernment, the true Light of the soul of Israel does not shine on him in all its illumination force, but only partially, by the measure he has purified himself by returning to the collective.

The sign for the body's complete correction is when one feels that one's soul exists in the whole of Israel, in each and every one of them, for which he does not feel himself as an individual, for one depends on the other. At that time, he is complete, flawless, and the soul truly shines on him in its fullest power, as it appeared in *Adam HaRishon*, as in "He who breathed, breathed from within Him."

This is the meaning of the three times of a person:

1.   A spark of a soul, the act by way of sparkling, as in prohibiting and permitting.

2.   A particular soul, one part out of 600,000. It is permanently completed, but its flaw is with it. This means that its body cannot receive the whole of the soul, and feels itself as being distinct, which causes him much pains of love.

Subsequently, he approaches perfection, the common soul, since the body has been cleansed and it is entirely dedicated to *HaVaYaH* and does not pose any measures and screens and is completely included in the whole of Israel. ... ...

We learned that "if even one man came before his Master in complete repentance, the Messiah King would come at once." It seems to mean, as they said (Song of Songs, 1), "Moses is equal to 600,000." We need to understand it, since this would mean that there are twice 600,000 souls—the soul of Moses and the soul of Israel.

But the truth is that there is no more than one soul, as it is known by the measure of each and every soul that purifies and cleanses itself from its filth. Hence, when all the souls are corrected, they will draw onto them the entire Higher soul of *Atzilut*, to each and every soul, since the spiritual is indivisible. At that time (Zechariah, 14:9) "And the Lord shall be King over all the earth." Hence, while even a single soul is denied of complete purity, the extension of *Kedusha* (Holiness) will be deficient in every soul from Israel.

And when a single soul from Israel is purified from all its filth, it will draw onto itself the whole of the soul of *Atzilut*, and through it, all the souls of its generation will be completed. This is the meaning of one being dependent on the other, as it is written (*Sanhedrin*, 11), "It was befitting that Divinity would be upon him, but his generation was unworthy of it."

The content of the words is unanimously bewildering, that the same soul that was rewarded with purification immediately strives to increase the grace of the generation and asks for them, until it elevates its entire generation to its merit.

This is the meaning of "Moses is equal to 600,000." Because he was their loyal shepherd, he had the same *Kedusha* (Holiness) that the whole generation had.

Indeed, the whole is found within each item, since in the end, all the souls will unite into one discernment, returning to their spiritual root. Hence, all the miracles and wonders and all the journeys they had travelled throughout the world during the 6,000 years should be experienced by each soul. The good soul draws to itself from all the discernments of *Kedusha* before it and after it; and the evil soul does to the contrary.

And the changing times are considered generations. However, each generation behaves as its judge, by the mind that judges it, since it receives from the *Kedusha* of that time.

For this reason, each soul is willing to draw the souls of Moses, Aaron, Samuel, David, and Solomon within it, as times that it experiences. During the exit from Egypt and the reception of the Torah, the soul of Moses appears on it; during the seven of the conquests, the souls of Joshua; and during the building of the Temple, the souls of King Solomon, etc.

This does not refer to the above-mentioned souls in particular, but according to the rule that we said that the spiritual is indivisible, as soon as one is rewarded with a soul, he is rewarded with the soul of the whole of Israel, though according to one's merit and place. Hence, at a time when one is rewarded with these wonders, one receives into himself the abundance of the soul in that disclosure, hence the name of the owner of that disclosure is upon him.

And they said (Shabbat, 67; *Baba Metzia*, 113), "All of Israel are sons of kings. Also (Jerusalem Talmud, *Masechet Horaiot* (Instructions), 3, 5), "A king that dies, all of Israel are worthy of kingship." This is a great secret, for in all the previous generations, which were but a preparation for *Malchut* (kingship), special *Kelim* (vessels) were required for anointment of their judges, such as the souls of Moses and Samuel. But the final purpose depends on the whole of Israel, since when a tiny part of a tiny spark is missing, the end will not be able to appear. Hence, all of Israel are worthy of kingship, since everyone is equal in this true discernment.

For this reason, there is no special *Kli* (vessel) for drawing that perfection, but anyone who cleanses and purifies his soul to be worthy of extending the revelation of *Malchut* in the world will literally be called "King David." This is the meaning of "David, King of Israel, is indeed alive," for he has not died at all. His *Kli* is within each and every soul from Israel. This is not the case with the soul of Moses, which is found only in the wise disciples in the generation, as well as in prophets and priests.

This is the meaning of (Jerusalem Talmud; *Masechet Horaiot*, 3, 5) "A king that dies, all of Israel are worthy of kingship." This is also the meaning of exempting the public.

This is the meaning of (*Sutah*, 49), "At the time of the Messiah, Chutzpah (impudence) will mount," and (Isaiah, 3:5) "the child shall behave insolently against the aged, and the base against the honorable." This means that even an ignoble child will dare to extend His kingship to the world, as though he were one of the elders and the honorable in the generation.

Should the ignoble, too—one who has a lowly and base soul at its root—aim his heart and purify his deeds to become worthy, he will be rewarded with extending the whole of the soul of a holy nation in his soul, with all the wonders that the holy nation has tasted thus far. This is because they were all but preparations for this wholeness.

Hence, even that particular soul must taste everything, and he will buy his world in an hour due to the ability of that generation to extend the crown of His kingship, which contains everything: "And all need the owner of the needles, and every element in it is required" (*Berachot*, 64; *Baba Batra*, 145).

This is the meaning of their words: "Even if one man came before his Master in complete repentance, the Messiah King would come at once." This means that whoever it was, even if it were only one man in the generation who was rewarded with extending that soul by himself, he will be able to reward his whole generation, since all who are obliged, exempt the public through their duty, and he can do much praying and hold his own until he rewards his entire generation.

This is not so with other kinds of redemptions, which were only in the form of preparations and did not belong to each and every one. For example, the giving of the Torah belongs specifically to the generation of the desert and to Moses. And any other generation, even if they were more worthy, did not extend that discernment, and neither did any other person besides Moses, for they were interdependent.

However, the Messiah is ready for each and every generation. Because of that, it is also ready for each and every person to extend the discernment of the Messiah, as in "All who are obliged," as mentioned above.

And the reason is that anointments concern the correction of the *Kelim*, and the portrayal of all the *Kelim* as equal, since any division between them is only in their *HBD*, by their measures. Hence, from the minister who sees the King's face to the one who sits behind the grindstone, all are equal servants in bringing back the old glory, and in that, there are no degrees between one another.

Not the Time for the Livestock to Be Gathered

"It is not the time for the livestock to be gathered. Water the sheep, and go, pasture them" (Genesis, 29:7). It is known that all the words of the righteous turn upwards, as it was said to him, "And it was revealed by the shepherds of Haran." It is so because it was impossible to roll the stone from the mouth of the well of the revealing of Rachel before all the herds were gathered and the stone was rolled off from the well's mouth.

In my humble opinion, it can be said that before each revelation, there must be covering, as in the darkness of the morning. For this reason, since Jacob arrived at the well of Rachel's revealing to Jacob, he did not feel Rachel's love as during the entire way, as he followed her with his cane through the Jordan.

This is why he set out for the upper well, for the well was blocked by the rock, and Jacob means elevating the externality. Hence, he set out to the externality. (This is the meaning of "And he sat on the well," meaning sitting.)

He promptly stood in prayer, and a man set out to the shepherds of the flock. (Why, etc.,) "It is not the time for the

251

livestock to be gathered. Water the sheep, and go, pasture them," as in (Song of Song, 1:7), "Where do you pasture," and "Where do you make it lie down." And the reply came to him, "We cannot, until all the flocks have gathered." That is, until Jacob achieves a coupling in externality, the whole of Israel, including the four mothers, are dependent on him alone. This is why his work was thus far alone, not in public, for he did not need any assistance from others and was the strongest in the work without ever being tired.

But at that moment, when it was his time to mate with Rachel to elicit seventy souls, he promptly felt weariness, and this is what he spoke and prayed about. (Indeed he knew) and this is the meaning of Jacob not rolling the stone from the well's mouth prior to the disclosure of Rachel. However, upon Rachel's disclosure before him, the *Zivug Eynaim* (coupling of the eyes) was completed. Therefore, at that time all of Israel were included in him. Thus, all the herds of that time had already gathered, and therefore, "[he] rolled the stone from the well's mouth."

But from then on, when the seventy souls of Jacob expanded into 600,000 souls, the matter returned to its initial state, requiring the gathering of all the herds in order to roll off the stone from the well's mouth. And when the power of one part is missing, it causes weakness in the whole level. This is the meaning of (Braita de Rabbi Ishmael) an individual that requires a collective, and anything that was in the collective and has departed the collective, does not testify to itself, but departed in order to testify to the entire collective, since (Psalms, 103:15) "As for man ... as a bud of the field, so he will bud."

The whole point of the buds rises into a single flower, the collective of Jacob and the tribes, a complete bed. This places a unique boundary for each and every soul, as in receiving light from above in this world, in the work, and one is greater than the other, one is higher than the other, and no face is like another.

The depiction of those boundaries is identical to the image of the lines and dots of the flower, where the boundaries in each part and dot on the flower form the beauty of the flower. But when the dot or the part in the flower extends its boundary, whether a little or a lot, it makes the whole flower unsightly. It is impossible to take only part of the flower and examine it alone, for then that part has neither beauty nor glory.

This is the meaning of the allegory in *The Zohar* (*The Sulam* commentary, Nasso, item 19) about two who boarded a boat, and one was drilling under him. His friend admonished him, "Why are you drilling?" And that fool replied, "Why should you care? I am drilling under me!" But indeed, the individual spoils the beauty of the entire image.

From this we understand that in the ruin of the First Temple, the craftsman and the locksmith did not save the Temple from ruin because the majority of their contemporaries spoiled the beauty, though in them there was no flaw, for prophecy is not present in a flawed place, not even in the slightest.

This is the meaning of a prayer in public, that one must not exclude oneself from the public and ask for oneself, not even to bring contentment to one's maker, but only for the entire public. It is so because one cannot extend one's boundary while the boundaries of the rest of the buds of the flower remain where they are, for as smallness blemishes the beauty, so does greatness, since the boundaries of all the lines and circles of the flower must be related.

This is the meaning of (Psalms, 22:21) "Save my soul from the sword, my only one from the dog." One who departs from the public to ask specifically for one's own soul does not build. On the contrary, he inflicts ruin upon his soul, as in (Midrash Rabah, Ch 7, item 6), "All who is proud," etc., for there cannot be one who retires from the public unless with an attire of pride. Woe unto him, for he inflicts ruin on his soul, for one who takes from the flower, not only does he condemn the beauty of the flower in general, that there is a flaw in their value, but even that specific part has no glory or beauty whatsoever, and no color in the eye will regard him.

For this reason, he ruins his soul, and also causes the giving of his *Yechida* (only one) to a dog, meaning *BON*, the parting of the points, while *MA* is the connection into a single flower, and *Yechida* is the one who receives the light of *MA*, and every person has a *Yechida*, meaning his own expansion.

This is what causes every boundary, meaning man's sensation of himself as a unique self, meaning an only one. Indeed, at the root, he is called *Yechida* (only one) because there, all the souls of Israel are only one, one collective, as in "counting a number and there is no number," and as in "collective and individual," as in choice. And all that is required of one's work is to extend upon himself the light of *Yechida*, which will be completed only when all the herds have gathered.

Even during work, when one prays alone, against his will he departs from the public and ruins his soul, which is from the *Chazeh* and below, as in the revealing and particularizing of the souls. Moreover, *Yechida* passes to the dog even at the root, as in the expanding of the name, *BON*, into (Isaiah, 56:10) "Dumb dogs cannot bark." That is, their cry will not rise to the heaven whatsoever, to the *Zivug* of *MA* and *BON*, meaning to unite, but is rather given to a dog, meaning the separation, as in *Hav! Hav!* (bark, but also "give" in Hebrew) of the daughters of Hell.

This is the meaning of (Exodus, 10:23) "And all the children of Israel had light in their dwellings," meaning their dwelling on the throne, which is from the *Chazeh* and below. It is a place where *Hassadim* are revealed and expand (for in *NHY*, the internality does not disappear and there are no intestines there), and also, "a dog will not bark" (Exodus, 11:7). That is, there was not even an awakening of anyone from the children of Israel to demand anything personal, as in *Hav! Hav!*, for no one needed anything because they did not feel as separate selves, and this was their power to come out of Egypt with a mighty hand.

Thus, every one must gather with all of one's strength into the whole of Israel with every plea to the Creator in the prayer and in the work, for it is insolence and great disgrace to disclose one's nakedness before, etc.

This is the meaning of (Exodus 20:23) "And you shall not go up by steps to My altar," meaning as an individual, where one is above the other. And especially that he desires to boast over the seed of holiness, and a holy nation does not need him. He marches on the heads of the holy nation and demands greatness over them. This is a disgrace we must not mention henceforth.

Instead, he should include himself in the only one, the root of all of Israel, as in (Isaiah, 44:6) "I am the first and I am the last." And then his strength is just as Jacob's strength. At that time he will be able to roll the stone from over the well's mouth with a mighty hand, and will water all the herds from a well of water, for the previous boundary will be lifted from all the souls of Israel, both below him and above him.

Moreover, the depictions of the boundaries of the flower that render glory and beauty will not change at all, for they will remain in their former depiction. But the boundary of the holiness in general will be expanded greatly, causing light to all the children of Israel in their dwellings. And then, even his own personal dog will remain dumb, for the light of beauty will appear, as in his dwelling place, meaning from the *Chazeh* and below, for so is the nature of the light of the collective that is on the individual who has been annulled with regard to his own individuality, and he does not feel himself.

Concealment and Disclosure of the Face of the Creator (A)

First concealment (depiction): His Face is not revealed; that is, the Creator does not behave toward a person according to His Name—The Good Who Does Good. Rather, it is to the contrary—one is afflicted by Him or suffers from poor income, and many people wish to collect their debts from him and make his life bitter. His whole day is filled with troubles and worries. Or, one suffers from poor health and disrespect from people. Every plan he begins, he fails to complete, and he is constantly dissatisfied.

In this manner, of course one does not see the Creator's Good Face, that is, if he believes that the Creator is the one who does these things to him, either as punishment for transgressions or to reward him in the end. This follows the verse, "Whom the Lord loves, He rebukes," and also, "The righteous begin with suffering, since the Creator wishes to eventually impart them great tranquility."

Yet, one does not fail in saying that all this came to him by blind fate and by nature without any reason and consideration. Rather, one strengthens in believing that the Creator, with His Guidance, caused him all that. This is nonetheless considered seeing the Creator's back.

Second concealment, which the books refer to as "concealment within concealment," means that one cannot see even the Creator's back. Instead, one says that the Creator has left him and no longer watches over him. He ascribes all the sufferings he feels to blind fate and to nature, since the ways of Providence become so complicated in one's eyes as to lead one to denial.

This means (depiction) that one prays and gives charity for one's troubles but is not answered whatsoever. And precisely when one stops praying for one's troubles, one is answered. Whenever he overcomes, believes in Providence, and makes his deeds good, luck turns away from him and he mercilessly falls back. And when he denies and begins to worsen his ways, he becomes very successful and is greatly relieved.

He does not find his sustenance in proper manners, but through deceit or desecration of the Sabbath. Or, all of his acquaintances who observe Torah and *Mitzvot* (commandments) suffer poverty, illness, and are despised by people. These observers of *Mitzvot* seem impolite to him, innately brainless, and so hypocritical that he cannot bear to be among them for even a minute.

Conversely, all his wicked acquaintances, who mock his faith, are very successful, well to do, and healthy. They know no sickness; they are clever, virtuous, and good-tempered. They are carefree, confident, and tranquil all day, every day.

When Providence arranges things in this manner for a person, it is called "concealment within concealment." This is because then one collapses under one's weight and cannot continue to strengthen the belief that one's pains come from the Creator for some hidden reason. Finally, one fails, becomes heretic, and says that the Creator is not watching over His creations whatsoever, and all that transpires, transpires by blind fate and nature. This is not seeing even the back.

Depiction of Disclosure of the Face

But once he has completely discovered the spice—the Light of Torah that one inhales into one's body—through strengthening in faith in the Creator, one becomes worthy of Guidance with His Face revealed. This means that the Creator behaves with him as is fitting to His Name, "The Good Who Does Good."

Thus (depiction), he receives abundant good and great tranquility from the Creator and is always satisfied. This is because one obtains one's livelihood with ease and to the fullest, never knows trouble or pressure, knows no illness, is highly respected by people, easily completes any plan that comes to his mind, and succeeds wherever he turns.

And when he wishes upon something, he prays and he is instantaneously answered, as He always answers anything that one demands of Him, and not a single prayer is denied. When one strengthens with good deeds, one succeeds even more, and when one is negligent, one's success proportionally decreases.

All of one's acquaintances are decent, of good income and health. They are highly respected in the eyes of people and have no worries at all. They are at peace all day and every day. They are smart, truthful, and so comely that one feels blessed and delighted to be among them.

Conversely, all of one's acquaintances who do not follow the path of Torah are of poor livelihood, troubled by heavy debts, and fail to find even a single moment's rest. They are sick, in pain, and despised by the people. They seem to him mindless, ill-mannered, wicked and cruel toward people, deceitful and such sycophants that it is intolerable to be among them.

His Name shows us that He is benevolent to all His creations in all the forms of benefit, sufficient for every kind of receiver from among Israel, for certainly, the pleasure of one is not like the pleasure of another. For example, one who engages in wisdom will not enjoy honor and wealth, and one who does not engage in wisdom will not enjoy great attainments and innovations in the wisdom. Thus, He gives wealth and honor to one, and wondrous attainments in the wisdom to another.

One's request to become stronger in believing in His Guidance over the world during the concealment period brings one to contemplate the books, the Torah, and to draw from there the illumination and the understanding how to strengthen one's faith in His Guidance. These illuminations and observations that one receives through the Torah are called "the spice of Torah." When they accumulate to a certain amount, the Creator has mercy on him and pours upon him the spirit from Above, that is, the Higher Abundance.

Concealment and Disclosure of the Face of the Creator (B)

DEPICTION OF CONCEALMENT OF THE FACE

1. Suffering torments such as deficient income, poor health, degradations, failing to accomplish plans, and dissatisfaction such as keeping oneself from tormenting one's friend.

2. Praying without being answered. Declining when bettering one's ways, and succeeding when worsening them. One's sustenance does not come in proper ways, but only by deception, stealing, or desecrating the Sabbath.

3. All of one's honest acquaintances suffer poverty, ill health, and degradations of all kinds, and one's wicked acquaintances mock him each day. They are successful, healthy, wealthy, and carefree.

4. All of his righteous acquaintances who keep Torah and *Mitzvot* seem cruel, egotistical, odd, or innately stupid and impolite, as well as hypocritical. He finds it repulsive to be with them, even in the Garden of Eden, and he cannot bear to be with them for even a moment.

DEPICTION OF DISCLOSURE OF THE FACE

1. Reception of abundant good and peace, obtainment of one's livelihood with ease and to the fullest. One never feels scarcity or ill health, he is respected wherever he turns, and successfully and easily accomplishes each plan that comes to his mind.

2. When one prays, he is immediately answered. When he betters his ways, he is very successful, and when he worsens his ways, he loses his success.

3. All one's acquaintances who walk on the straight path are wealthy, healthy, know no illness, are highly respected by people, and dwell in peace and tranquility. And acquaintances who do not follow the straight path are of poor income, filled with troubles and pains, ill, and contemptible in the eyes of people.

4. One regards all the righteous acquaintances as clever, reasonable, well-mannered, truthful, and so comely that it is most pleasurable to be among them.

Further Reading

The Secrets of the Eternal Book

The Five Books of Moses (The Torah) are part of the all-time bestselling book, The Bible. Ironically, the Bible is an encoded text. Beneath it lies another level, a hidden subtext that describes the ascent of humanity toward its highest level—the attainment of the Creator.

The Secrets of the Eternal Book decodes some of the Bible's most enigmatic, yet oft-cited epochs, such as the story of Creation, and the Children of Israel's exodus from Egypt.

The author's lively and easygoing style makes for a smooth entrance into the deepest level of reality, where one changes one's world simply by contemplation and desire.

The Kabbalah Experience

The depth of the wisdom revealed in the questions and answers within this book will inspire readers to reflect and contemplate. This is not a book to race through, but rather one that should be read thoughtfully and carefully. With this approach, readers will begin to experience a growing sense of enlightenment while simply absorbing the answers to the questions every Kabbalah student asks along the way.

The Kabbalah Experience is a guide from the past to the future, revealing situations that all students of Kabbalah will experience at some point along their journeys. For those who cherish every moment in life, this book offers unparalleled insights into the timeless wisdom of Kabbalah.

The Path of Kabbalah

This unique book combines beginners' material with more advanced concepts and teachings. If you have read a book or two of Laitman's, you will find this book very easy to relate to.

While touching upon basic concepts such as perception of reality and Freedom of Choice, *The Path of Kabbalah* goes deeper and expands beyond the scope of beginners' books. The structure of the worlds, for example, is explained in greater detail here than in the "pure" beginners' books. Also described is the spiritual root of mundane matters such as the Hebrew calendar and the holidays.

The Book of Zohar: annotations to the Ashlag commentary

The Book of Zohar is an age-old source of wisdom and the basis for all Kabbalistic literature. Since its appearance, it has been the primary, and often only source used by Kabbalists.

Written in a unique and metaphorical language, *The Book of Zohar* enriches our understanding of reality and widens our worldview. Rav Yehuda Ashlag's unique *Sulam* (Ladder) commentary allows us to grasp the hidden meanings of the text and "climb" toward the lucid perceptions and insights that the book holds for those who study it.

Attaining the Worlds Beyond

From the introduction to Attaining the Worlds Beyond: "...Not feeling well on the Jewish New Year's Eve of September 1991, my teacher called me to his bedside and handed me his notebook, saying, 'Take it and learn from it.' The following morning, he perished in my arms, leaving me and many of his other disciples without guidance in this world.

"He used to say, 'I want to teach you to turn to the Creator, rather than to me, because He is the only strength, the only Source of all that exists, the only one who can really help you, and He awaits your prayers for help. When you seek help in your search for freedom from the bondage of this world, help in elevating yourself above this world, help in finding the self, and help in determining your purpose in life, you must turn to the Creator, who sends you all those aspirations in order to compel you to turn to Him.'"

Attaining the Worlds Beyond holds within it the content of that notebook, as well as other inspiring texts. This book reaches out to all those seekers who want to find a logical, reliable way to understand the world we live in. This fascinating introduction to the wisdom of Kabbalah will enlighten the mind, invigorate the heart, and move readers to the depths of their souls.

The Wise Heart: Tales and allegories
by three contemporary sages

Kabbalah students and enthusiasts in Kabbalah often wonder what the spiritual world actually feels like to a Kabbalist. *The Wise Heart* is a lovingly crafted anthology comprised of tales and allegories by Kabbalist Dr. Michael Laitman, his mentor, Rav Baruch Ashlag (Rabash), and Rabash's father and mentor, Rav Yehuda Ashlag, author of the acclaimed *Sulam* (Ladder) commentary on *The Book of Zohar*. The poems herein offer surprising and often amusing depictions of human nature, with a loving and tender touch that is truly unique to Kabbalists.

Shamati (I Heard)

Rav Michael Laitman's words on the book: "Among all the texts and notes that were used by my teacher, Rav Baruch Shalom Halevi Ashlag (the Rabash), there was one special notebook he always carried. This notebook contained transcripts of his conversations with his father, Rav Yehuda Leib Halevi Ashlag (Baal HaSulam), author of the *Sulam* (Ladder) commentary on *The Book of Zohar*, *The Study of the Ten Sefirot* (a commentary on the texts of the Kabbalist, Ari), and many other works on Kabbalah.

"Not feeling well on the Jewish New Year's Eve of September 1991, the Rabash summoned me to his bedside and handed me a notebook, whose cover contained only one word, *Shamati* (I Heard). As he handed the notebook, he said, 'Take it and learn from it.' The following morning, my teacher perished in my arms, leaving me and many of his other disciples without guidance in this world.

Committed to Rabash's legacy to disseminate the wisdom of Kabbalah, I published the notebook just as it was written, thus retaining the text's transforming powers. Among all the books of Kabbalah, *Shamati* is a unique and compelling creation."

Kabbalah for the Student

Kabbalah for the Student offers authentic texts by Rav Yehuda Ashlag, author of the *Sulam* (Ladder) commentary on *The Book of Zohar*, his son and successor, Rav Baruch Ashlag, as well as other great Kabbalists. It also offers illustrations that accurately depict the evolution of the Upper Worlds as Kabbalists experience them. The book also contains several explanatory essays that help us understand the texts within.

In *Kabbalah for the Student*, Rav Michael Laitman, PhD, Rav Baruch Ashlag's personal assistant and prime student, compiled all the texts a Kabbalah student would need in order to attain the spiritual worlds. In his daily lessons, Rav Laitman bases his teaching on these inspiring texts, thus helping novices and veterans alike to better understand the spiritual path we undertake on our fascinating journey to the Higher Realms.

Rabash—the Social Writings

Rav Baruch Shalom HaLevi Ashlag (Rabash) played a remarkable role in the history of Kabbalah. He provided us with the necessary final link connecting the wisdom of Kabbalah to our human experience. His father and teacher was the great Kabbalist, Rav Yehuda Leib HaLevi Ashlag, known as Baal HaSulam for his *Sulam* (Ladder) commentary on *The Book of Zohar*. Yet, if not for the essays of Rabash, his father's efforts to disclose the wisdom of Kabbalah to all would have been in vain. Without those essays, few would be able to achieve the spiritual attainment that Baal HaSulam so desperately wanted us to obtain.

The writings in this book aren't just for reading. They are more like an experiential user's guide. It is very important to work with them in order to see what they truly contain. The reader should try to put them into practice by living out the emotions Rabash so masterfully describes. He always advised his students to summarize the articles, to work with the texts, and those who attempt it discover that it always yields new insights. Thus, readers are advised to work with the texts, summarize them, translate them, and implement them in the group. Those who do so will discover the power in the writings of Rabash.

Gems of Wisdom: words of the great Kabbalists from all generations

Through the millennia, Kabbalists have bequeathed us with numerous writings. In their compositions, they have laid out a structured method that can lead, step by step, unto a world of eternity and wholeness.

Gems of Wisdom is a collection of selected excerpts from the writings of the greatest Kabbalists from all generations, with particular emphasis on the writings of Rav Yehuda Leib HaLevi Ashlag (Baal HaSulam), author of the *Sulam* [Ladder] commentary of *The Book of Zohar*.

The sections have been arranged by topics, to provide the broadest view possible on each topic. This book is a useful guide to any person desiring spiritual advancement.

Let There Be Light: selected excerpts from The Book of Zohar

The Zohar contains all the secrets of Creation, but until recently the wisdom of Kabbalah was locked under a thousand locks. Thanks to the work of Rav Yehuda Ashlag (1884-1954), the last of the great Kabbalists, The Zohar is revealed today in order to propel humanity to its next degree.

Let There Be Light contains selected excerpts from the series Zohar for All, a refined edition of The Book of Zohar with the Sulam commentary. Each piece was carefully chosen for its beauty and depth as well as its capacity to draw the reader into The Zohar and get the most out of the reading experience. As The Zohar speaks of nothing but the intricate web that connects all souls, diving into its words attracts the special force that exists in that state of oneness, where we are all connected.

The Science of Kabbalah

Kabbalist and scientist Rav Michael Laitman, PhD, designed this book to introduce readers to the special language and terminology of the authentic wisdom of Kabbalah. Here, Rav Laitman reveals authentic Kabbalah in a manner both rational and mature. Readers are gradually led to understand the logical design of the Universe and the life that exists in it.

The Science of Kabbalah, a revolutionary work unmatched in its clarity, depth, and appeal to the intellect, will enable readers to approach the more technical works of Baal HaSulam (Rabbi Yehuda Ashlag), such as The Study of the Ten Sefirot and The Book of Zohar. Readers of this book will enjoy the satisfying answers to the riddles of life that only authentic Kabbalah provides. Travel through the pages and prepare for an astonishing journey into the Upper Worlds.

Introduction to the Book of Zohar

This volume, along with *The Science of Kabbalah*, is a required preparation for those who wish to understand the hidden message of *The Book of Zohar*. Among the many helpful topics dealt with in this text is an introduction to the "language of roots and branches," without which the stories in *The Zohar* are mere fable and legend. Introduction to *The Book of Zohar* will provide readers with the necessary tools to understand authentic Kabbalah as it was originally meant to be—as a means to attain the Upper Worlds.

The Kabbalist: a cinematic novel

At the dawn of the deadliest era in human history, the 20th century, a mysterious man appeared carrying a stern warning for humanity and an unlikely solution to its suffering. In his writings, Kabbalist Yehuda Ashlag described in clarity and great detail the wars and upheavals he foresaw, and even more strikingly, the current economic, political, and social crises we are facing today. His deep yearning for a united humanity has driven him to unlock *The Book of Zohar* and make it—and the unique force contained therein—accessible to all.

The Kabbalist is a cinematic novel that will turn on its head everything you thought you knew about Kabbalah, spirituality, freedom of will, and our perception of reality. The book carries a message of unity with scientific clarity and poetic depth. It transcends religion, nationality, mysticism, and the fabric of space and time to show us that the only miracle is the one taking place within, when we begin to act in harmony with Nature and with the entire humanity.

The Writings of the Last Generation & The Nation

In 1940, Rav Yehuda Ashlag, author of the *Sulam* (ladder) commentary on *The Book of Zohar*, published the first copy of the paper, *The Nation*. Alas, obstacles had caused the first issue to also be the only issue ever to be printed.

After WWII, Rav Ashlag wrote *The Writings of the Last Generation*, where he contemplates the causes and solutions to anti-Semitism. In this book, we have published both these writings and *The Nation*. Even today these writings are bold, inspiring, and truly make you wonder what our world would be like had we known about them decades ago.

CONTACT INFORMATION

1057 Steeles Avenue West, Suite 532
Toronto, ON, M2R 3X1
Canada

Bnei Baruch USA,
2009 85th street, #51,
Brooklyn, New York, 11214
USA

E-mail: info@kabbalah.info
Web site: www.kabbalah.info

Toll free in USA and Canada:
1-866-LAITMAN
Fax: 1-905 886 9697